CHRIST'S RETURN AND TODAY'S GLOBAL GEOPOLITICAL BOMBSHELLS

CHRIST'S RETURN AND TODAY'S GLOBAL GEOPOLITICAL BOMBSHELLS

Understanding What Might Take Place After This

Dr. David F. Liang
with Dorothy Liang

ELM HILL

A Division of
HarperCollins Christian Publishing

www.elmhillbooks.com

Christ's Return and Today's Global Geopolitical Bombshells
Understanding What Might Take Place After This

Published in Nashville, Tennessee, by Elm Hill, an imprint of Thomas Nelson. Elm Hill and Thomas Nelson are registered trademarks of HarperCollins Christian Publishing, Inc.

Elm Hill titles may be purchased in bulk for educational, business, fund-raising, or sales promotional use. For information, please e-mail SpecialMarkets@ ThomasNelson.com.

Library of Congress Cataloging-in-Publication Data

Library of Congress Control Number: 2019931460

Prelaunch ISBN: 978-0-310102038

ISBN 978-0-310102045 (Paperback)
ISBN 978-0-310102052 (Hardbound)
ISBN 978-0-310102069 (eBook)

CONTENTS

PREFACE

A mong so-called holy books, the Bible is unique in its two-thousand-year-old declaration: "Come up here, and I will show you what must take place after this" (Revelation 4:1). This prophetic invitation set this principal author on a lifelong effort to study what might happen after this in the context of global geopolitics—and to share his hypotheses in this book. Amazingly, a variety of headline-grabbing global bombshells surrounding the denuclearization of North Korea, Brexit, Israel, Iran, China, Russia, and the presidency of Donald Trump can each be understood in terms of ancient Bible prophecies.

This principal author cherishes the tremendous opportunity he had working in the research and development branch of Canada's Department of National Defence[1] (DND) for twenty-seven years. As he gradually took on greater responsibility—including representing Canada in dealing with the US through the North American Aerospace Defense Command (NORAD), National Reconnaissance Office (NRO), Central Intelligence Agency (CIA) and Ballistic Missile Defense Organization (BMDO) as well as dealing with allies from NATO (North Atlantic Treaty Organization)—he became ever more conscious of Bible prophecies unfolding in terms of global geopolitics and military defence.

In the 1980s, while crisscrossing Europe to attend NATO-related functions, this principal author's attention was drawn to what might

---

[1]   Note for US readers: Canada spells defence with a c, not an s.

take place in Europe, especially Germany. Having grown up in Indonesia and having been exposed to events in North and South Vietnam, China and Taiwan, as well as North and South Korea, amongst others, he became fascinated with Daniel chapter 2 in the Bible, which seemed to prophesy the unification of divided countries (like mixtures of iron and clay). He wrote in 1988 and published in May 1989 his hypotheses that Germany might unify; that the US might withdraw from the European political arena; and that China's military and intellectuals would enter into conflict.

To his surprise, in May 2000, a decade after his ideas were published, the report from the US National Reconnaissance Office (NRO), *Proteus: Insights from 2020*, forecasted scenarios for the year 2020 that overlapped with his analyses. Back in the 1980s, it was almost lunacy to speculate that Germany would unify. Even after the Berlin Wall's 1989 collapse, reconciliation between North and South Korea or between China and Taiwan remained implausible. But his insight came from the careful study of Bible prophecy.

Bible prophecies about the end times can help us understand what happens around the globe. With this book, this principal author has worked with his daughter's resourceful support to address—through the lens of Bible prophecy—the possibilities of the US retreating; the Koreas unifying; Russia, China, and Israel rising; the emergence of a ten-king European coalition; turmoil in the Middle East; and ultimately the rise of the Antichrist.

Two millennia ago, the Bible accurately prophesied modern-day geopolitical bombshells. This evidence of the Bible's supernatural authority gives us reason to believe in other Biblical contents—including the promised return of Jesus Christ. Amen. Come, Lord Jesus!

CHAPTER 1

THE END OF THE WORLD BOMBSHELL

Stephen Hawking's End of the World Bombshell

I n March 2018, two weeks before his death, Stephen Hawking and a coauthor finalized an article predicting that the universe would end by fading into darkness when the stars run out of energy. They submitted the article titled "A Smooth Exit from Eternal Inflation" to a leading scientific journal.[2]

Almost a year earlier, on 5 May 2017, CNBC reported: "Stephen Hawking says humans must colonize another planet in 100 years or face extinction."[3] According to the article:

> With climate change, overdue asteroid strikes, epidemics and population growth, our own planet is increasingly precarious.

---

[2] Jonathan Leake, 2018 March 18, "Stephen Hawking's parting shot is multi-cosmic," https://www.thetimes.co.uk/article/stephen-hawkings-parting-shot-is-multi-cosmic-nbg0t6t9j

[3] Arjun Kharpal, 2017 May 5, "Stephen Hawking says humans must colonize another planet in 100 years or face extinction," https://www.cnbc.com/2017/05/05/stephen-hawking-human-extinction-colonize-planet.html

Previously, Hawking theorized that humanity probably has around 1,000 years left before it becomes extinct. His timeline appears now to have shortened.

"Although the chance of a disaster to planet Earth in a given year may be quite low, it adds up over time, and becomes a near certainty in the next thousand or ten thousand years," Hawking told the BBC in an interview at the time.

The *Chicago Tribune* also reported on the 100-year deadline:[4]

In recent months, Hawking has been explicit about humanity's need to find a "Planet B." In the past, he has also called for humans to colonize the moon and find a way to settle Mars—a locale he referred to as "the obvious next target" in 2008, according to *New Scientist* [magazine].

"We must ... continue to go into space for the future of humanity...."

"I don't think we will survive another 1,000 years without escaping beyond our fragile planet."

Sir Martin Rees and Others

Hawking was not alone in making dire predictions for our planet. Sir Martin Rees was the fifty-ninth president of the Royal Society—effectively Britain's 'top scientist.' He was also a master of Trinity College, Cambridge, and has been the astronomer royal since 1995. Rees published a book in 2003 entitled: *Our Final Hour: A Scientist's Warning: How Terror, Error, and Environmental Disaster Threaten Humankind's Future In This Century—On Earth and Beyond.*

---

[4] Peter Holley, 2017 May 5, "Stephen Hawking now says humanity has only about 100 years to escape Earth," www.chicagotribune.com/news/nationworld/science/ct-stephen-hawking-escape-earth-20170505-story.html

In this book, he discusses a range of existential risks confronting humanity, and controversially estimates that humanity has a mere 50/50 chance of surviving beyond the year 2100 CE. Sir Martin Rees is so concerned with these terrible prospects for mother earth that he has cofounded an apocalypse think tank called Center for the Study of Existential Risk.

Eminent Australian scientist Frank Fenner, who helped to wipe out smallpox, predicts humans (and many other creatures) "will become extinct, perhaps within 100 years," because of the massive scale of human impact on the Earth (overpopulation, environmental destruction, and climate change). He believes the situation is irreversible, and it is too late for humans to change course.[5]

In February 2018, the British newspaper *Daily Mail* reported: "Underwater supervolcano could erupt without warning and kill 100 million people after scientists find a 6-mile wide lava dome growing off the coast of Japan."[6] Referring to a study conducted by Kobe University (Japan) researchers, the article stated:

> A submerged volcano off the coast of Japan that erupted 7,300 years ago could be preparing to make a comeback. Scientists have discovered evidence of a giant dome of lava in the Kikai volcano's collapsed magma chamber....
>
> Currently the dome is around 6.2 miles (10 kilometers) wide and 1,968 feet (600 meters) tall. Scientists say an eruption could take place without warning, and if it does, it could kill as many as 100 million people and trigger a 'volcanic winter.'

---

5   Cheryl Jones, 2010 June 16, "Frank Fenner sees no hope for humans," https://www.theaustralian.com.au/higher-education/frank-fenner-sees-no-hope-for-humans/news-story/8d77f0806a8a3591d47013f7d75699b9

6   Cecile Borkhataria, 2018 February 13, "Underwater supervolcano could erupt without warning and kill 100 million people after scientists find a 6-mile wide lava dome growing off the coast of Japan," http://www.dailymail.co.uk/sciencetech/article-5384899/Lava-building-volcano-near-Japans-southerly-islands.html

However, the research paper said, "Such supereruptions are 'rare but extremely hazardous events.'"

Doomsday utterances or scientific reports by these scientific and scholastic heavyweights affirm that this mother earth cannot subsist much longer. This leaves room for what many Christians foresee as the second coming of Christ, when he returns to earth and fully establishes his kingdom here. The planet's 'reboot' would be unnecessary if mankind were able to resolve all the problems facing mankind and this mother earth.

Isaac Newton

Isaac Newton was arguably the greatest scientist who ever lived. His book *Mathematical Principles of Natural Philosophy*, published in 1687, remains a most powerful and influential scientific treatise that has dominated scientists' views of the physical universe for the last three centuries. In 2005 when a survey of scientists in the UK-based Royal Society asked whether Newton or Albert Einstein had the greater effect on the history of science, Newton was deemed the more influential one.[7]

Though he is known for his scientific insights, biblical hermeneutics was Newton's greatest passion. He devoted more time to the study of Scripture than to science, and he said: "I have a fundamental belief in the Bible as the Word of God, written by those who were inspired. I study the Bible daily."[8]

In June 2007, the National Museum in Jerusalem publicly displayed some of Newton's religiously-interested manuscripts. In a manuscript written in 1704, Newton attempted to collect scientific information

---

[7]   2005 November 23, "Newton beats Einstein in polls of scientists and the public," https://royalsociety.org/news/2012/newton-einstein/

[8]   John Hudson Tiner, 2006, *Exploring the World of Physics: From Simple Machines to Nuclear Energy* (Master Books) p.30

from the book of Daniel. Newton concluded that the world would end no earlier than 2060. In predicting this he stated:

> This I mention not to assert when the time of the end shall be, but to put a stop to the rash conjectures of fanciful men who are frequently predicting the time of the end, and by doing so bring the sacred prophesies [*sic*] into discredit as often as their predictions fail.[9]

That was not the only time when Newton criticized people who had given prophecy a bad name by trying to predict the future. In *Observations upon the Prophecies of Daniel and the Apocalypse of St. John*, which was published in 1733 after his death, Newton wrote:

> The folly of Interpreters has been, to foretel[*sic*] times and things by this Prophecy [the book of Revelation], as if God designed to make them Prophets.... The design of God was much otherwise. He gave this and the Prophecies of the Old Testament, not to gratify men's curiosities by enabling them to foreknow things, but that after they were fulfilled they might be interpreted by the event, and his own Providence, not the Interpreters['s], be then manifested thereby to the world.[10]

God's prophecies were intended to increase men's faith. That is consistent with Jesus's words in John 13:19: "From now on I am telling you before it comes to pass, so that when it does occur, you may believe that I am He" (New American Standard Bible).

Elsewhere, Newton interpreted biblical prophecies to mean that the

---

[9] See for example Matti Friedman, 2007 June 19, "Papers Reveal Isaac Newton's Religious Side," https://www.livescience.com/1638-papers-reveal-isaac-newton-religious-side.html

[10] Isaac Newton, 1733, *Observations upon the Prophecies of Daniel and the Apocalypse of St. John*, Part II (Observations upon the Apocalypse of St. John), end of Chapter 1

Jews would return to the Holy Land before the world ends. This is discussed in Chapter 4.

One of the curators of the manuscript exhibit in 2007 reportedly said that this area of Newton's writings "complicate[s] the idea that science is diametrically opposed to religion." These writings "show a scientist guided by religious fervor, by a desire to see God's actions in the world."[11]

Failed Doomsday Prophecies

Throughout the ages, men have made failed doomsday prophecies such as the Great Fire of London of 1666, the Mormon Armageddon of '1891 or earlier,' the Halley's Comet panic of 1910, Michael Nostradamus's prediction regarding August 1999, the Y2K computer bug of January 1, 2000, the Mayan Apocalypse of 2012, etc. People the world over are eager to believe in the predictions of Nostradamus and the Mayas while dismissing the Bible's predictions.

Faced with so many failures of nonbiblical doomsday prophecies, it is reasonable to question whether the Bible's end-time prophecies are any more reliable. Each of the other predictive failures was hinged on one specific artifact, one specific quote or one specific threat that pointed to a predicted doomsday.

In contrast, the Bible contains a broad spectrum of specific prophecies that can be examined on their own respective merits—therefore there could have been a multitude of possible points of failure to destroy the Bible's credibility. The aim of this book is to examine specific but broadly-based Bible prophecies, particularly in view of today's global geopolitical dynamics in the United States, Russia, North Korea, Britain, Europe, the Middle East (including Israel, Turkey, and Iran) and China.

How could it be possible that today's geopolitical dynamics around

---

[11] Matti Friedman, 2007 June 19, "Papers Reveal Isaac Newton's Religious Side," https://www.livescience.com/1638-papers-reveal-isaac-newton-religious-side.html

the world are precisely predicted in Bible prophecies written some two to three millennia ago? The Bible states: "All scripture is given by inspiration of God" (2 Timothy 3:16, King James Version). The more individual prophecies are found to be accurate and therefore credible, the more we can be assured that all scripture is truly given by God's inspiration. And we can begin to understand why Newton, as noted above, said, "I have a fundamental belief in the Bible as the Word of God, written by those who were inspired. I study the Bible daily."

CHAPTER 2

THE YANKEE GOING HOME BOMBSHELL

The Triumph of Liberal Democracy

In the summer of 1989 as the Soviet Union was disintegrating, the American magazine *The National Interest* published an essay boldly titled "The End of History?"[12] Its author, political scientist Francis Fukuyama, declared that the great ideological battles between East and West were over, and that Western liberal democracy had triumphed.

Fukuyama believed that Western liberal democracy, with its elegant balance of liberty and equality, could not be bettered; that its attainment would lead to a general calming in world affairs; and that in the long run it would be the only credible game in town.[13] Fukuyama wrote:

---

[12] Francis Fukuyama, "The End of History?" in *The National Interest* No. 16 (Summer 1989), pp. 3-1 , https://www.jstor.org/stable/24027184

See also Eliane Glaser, 2014 March 21, "Bring back ideology: Fukuyama's 'end of history' 25 years on," https://www.theguardian.com/books/2014/mar/21/bring-back-ideology-fukuyama-end-history-25-years-on

[13] Eliane Glaser, *ibid.*

"What we may be witnessing is not just the end of the Cold War, or the passing of a particular period of postwar history, but the end of history as such: that is, the end point of mankind's ideological evolution and the universalization of Western liberal democracy as the final form of human government."[14]

In 1999, *Foreign Affairs* magazine published a similarly-captivating article entitled "The Lonely Superpower" by renowned Harvard Professor Samuel P. Huntington.[15] He perceived the United States as the "lonely superpower" that decisively won the Cold War. He asserted: "The United States, of course, is the sole state with preeminence in every domain of power—economic, military, diplomatic, ideological, technological, and cultural—with the reach and capabilities to promote its interests in virtually every part of the world."[16]

What Must Take Place After This

Meanwhile, in 1988 the chief editor of *Proclaim Magazine*, a prominent Chinese Christian publication from the US-based Chinese Christian Mission, invited this principal author to write about the tumultuous situations around the world as seen through the lens of Bible prophecies. At that time, this principal author had been talking about current global affairs and Bible prophecies for more than ten years mostly among Chinese audiences. He had taken a strong interest in Bible prophecies ever since he became a Christian in January 1967. Soon afterward, aside from studying engineering he started spending much of his time reading and studying the Bible, and kneeling in front of God in prayer. One day as he read Revelation 4:1, he was electrified with this verse (in the New

---

[14] Fukuyama, *ibid*. p.4

[15] Samuel P. Huntington, "The Lonely Superpower" in *Foreign Affairs* Vol. 78, No. 2 (Mar.–Apr., 1999), pp. 35–49, http://www.jstor.org/stable/20049207

[16] Huntington, *ibid*. p. 36

International Version): "And the voice I had first heard speaking to me like a trumpet said, 'Come up here, and I will show you what must take place after this.'"

What an amazing promise! "I will show you what must take place." It meant, in other words: "I will show you with 100 percent certainty what will take place after this."

Later as this principal author was hired into Canadian defence research and development (R&D), he began working on missile guidance and control. He started having access to plenty of classified information in the "black" world. This further enhanced his interest in keeping one hand on the Bible and the other hand looking for information that could explain or substantiate what the Bible was saying in terms of "what must take place."

Thereafter, as he consolidated his understanding of Bible prophecies and whatever other sources of information he could get, he started to formulate geopolitical prognoses that could unfold in the future. So he wrote in 1988, and *Proclaim Magazine* published in May 1989 in Chinese, forecasting that:

- the US would ultimately withdraw from the European political arena, leaving Europe to the Europeans and leading to the appearance of a "ten-king coalition"[17];
- the Soviet Union's glasnost[18] East-West peace dialogue could cascade into the unification of East and West Germany; and
- conflict would arise in China between intellectuals and the military, leading to calamity for the intellectuals.

---

[17] Daniel chapter 7 describe's Daniels vision of a ten-horned beast representing ten nations. This will be further discussed in Chapter 8.

[18] See for example "The Gorbachev era: perestroika and glasnost," https://www.britannica.com/place/Russia/The-Gorbachev-era-perestroika-and-glasnost

Looking back into the geopolitical reality of 1988, each of the above three possibilities seemed far-fetched. These possibilities are not known to have crossed the fine minds of any political pundits of the time. It was highly improbable that these three possibilities would ever come true. But against all odds, at least two of these possibilities already came true in 1989-1990.

The US's Position in End-Time Prophecy

So what led this principal author to go against the grain of these political scientists' fascination with the US's unprecedented ascendance to the status of a 'lonely superpower'?

Certainly the US dominated much of the twentieth century's geopolitics, as Britain had dominated much of the nineteenth century. However, in the wealth of Biblical prophecies there is scarcely a mention of the US except perhaps in Ezekiel 38:13:

> Sheba, and Dedan, and the merchants of Tarshish, with all the young lions thereof, shall say unto thee, Art thou come to take a spoil? hast thou gathered thy company to take a prey? to carry away silver and gold, to take away cattle and goods, to take a great spoil? (King James Version)

Here Ezekiel describes an invasion of Israel that will be launched in the end times by a nation *"from the remote parts of the north."* Geographically, this could be Russia.

The KJV's reference to "young lions" (to be contrasted with "villages," "leaders," and "rulers" in other translations) lends itself to an imaginative interpretation; the lion has historically been a symbol of Great Britain, so other countries such as the US, Canada, Australia, and New Zealand, could plausibly fit into the concept of "young lions."

However, Bible prophecy scholar Dr. Hal Lindsey pointed out:

But this doesn't work, either. First and foremost, nobody can pinpoint with any degree of accuracy the location of Tarshish. The only thing we are sure of is that it isn't Britain. The most recent archeological evidence puts ancient Tarshish in Spain, which, while close, doesn't quite win the cigar.[19]

Even if the US fits into this prophetic passage of Ezekiel, the US's role in the prophecy amounts to nothing more than a verbal protest against invasion and looting by a northern country (possibly Russia). Such a role hardly befits the US's profile as a 'lonely superpower.'

Dr. Hal Lindsey had this to say: "I personally believe that one explanation could be that our country and its leadership will be so decimated following the rapture that we will simply cease to be a major influence overnight."[20]

This principal author agrees with Dr. Lindsey that when the rapture comes and all Christians in the US, from hopefully the president and congressional leaders to Christians through all echelons of US society (political, economic, civilian, military, and social) suddenly disappear; the US government and all civilian institutions will be so decimated that the US will suddenly become like a developing nation incapable of having much influence on the global scene.

Proteus: Insights from 2020

The prediction of a US decline and withdrawal from the European political arena got an unlikely boost from a study conducted by the US's National Reconnaissance Office (NRO) between 1999 and 2000, called *Proteus: Insights from 2020*. The NRO led the US's intelligence community in conducting this study aimed at prognosticating the future global geostrategic landscape and its characteristics out to 2020. A

---

[19] Hal Lindsey, 2001, "America in Prophecy," http://www.wnd.com/2001/05/9070/

[20] Hal Lindsey, 2001, "America in Prophecy," http://www.wnd.com/2001/05/9070/

1996 bipartisan US Congressional Commission report[21] noted that the NRO had the largest budget of any member of the intelligence community.[22] In the preface to *Proteus: Insights from 2020*, David A. Kier, the then-deputy director of NRO, commented:

> The *Proteus* Insights are the result of nearly 18 months of effort involving some of the best minds in the country—from poets to intelligence professionals—brought together by the National Reconnaissance Office to examine how we might come to grips with the future.[23]

He continued: "For me, there were some major surprises in the findings, and I have directed the team to continue its work." This principal author can only speculate that Kier might have been most surprised by the bombshell future-world scenario labelled "Yankee Going Home."

Yankee Going Home Bombshell

As one of "five plausible future worlds,"[24] Yankee Going Home would see the US withdrawing from the world after a series of foreign policy blunders and a deep economic recession. The Proteus Project came up with this bombshell scenario at the height of US geopolitical supremacy around the world, when no other country seemed able to challenge the US's status as the world's only superpower. Notably, this scenario was forecasted after the US's decisive victory in the Cold War against the Soviet Union; before the crippling effects of the 9/11 attacks; before the

---

[21] Commission on the Roles and Capabilities of the United States Intelligence Community; report entitled "Preparing for the 21st Century: An Appraisal of US Intelligence" https://www.gpo.gov/fdsys/pkg/GPO-INTELLIGENCE/content-detail.html

[22] *Ibid.* chapter 13, p.132

[23] *Proteus: Insights from 2020*, 2000 Copernicus Institute, page vii

[24] *Proteus: Insights from 2020*, page 8

US's disastrous venture in attacking Iraq; and long before the economic crisis of 2008-2009.

The Yankee Going Home scenario from *Proteus: Insights from 2020* was as follows:

Who runs things? Why are decisions made and what goals are being pursued? Who are our friends and our enemies? Just what is going on in the world? In 2020 you could be forgiven asking those questions because little is clear except that the world has changed in fundamental ways. The US has withdrawn from the world, gone home, after a series of terrible foreign policy blunders and a long-standing and deep recession. The world is heavily influenced by the memories of terrorism, war, and instability that followed US isolationism. In the wake of the US retreat, we find a world made up of both traditional actors (nations, international organizations) and powerful non-traditional actors (global corporate alliances, criminal groups, mercenary units). They cooperate for power and influence and compete for position and control in a shifting calliope of politics and economics that is bewildering to nearly all. In this world, traditional notions of allegiance are questioned and the "rules of the game" are difficult to understand.[25]

Subsequent to its publication in 2000, part of this Yankee Going Home scenario has been borne out in recent global geopolitical and economic events related to the US.

In terms of a long-standing and deep economic recession, the scenario forecasted that:

- Leading up to 2007, the US was in a downward spiral. The country looked foolish and ineffective to the world. It was

---

[25] *Proteus: Insights from 2020* page F-i

therefore not surprising that the instability hit the stock markets hard; investors were losing confidence. By February 2007, the Dow Jones Industrial Average (DJIA) was down to 16,000, having lost 15 percent of its value. Capital was fleeing abroad, mostly to Asia and Latin America. A recession hit hard and by June 2007 unemployment was up to 12 percent. The mood of the American voter became increasingly insecure and angry. By the end of the year, it was clear that no one would win the next presidential election unless they sponsored isolationist policies.

The DJIA did not fall in February 2007, as the scenario imagined. But it fell shortly thereafter; on September 29, 2008, the Dow fell 778 points or 7 percent. That record-breaking single-day drop was consistent with the Project Proteus prediction from eight years earlier!

In terms of the US military posture around the world, the Yankee Going Home scenario forecasted that:

- US armed forces and their prepositioned equipment were brought home. The US defense budget was cut by 20 percent. Across the world, the 'police' everyone had taken for granted went home. Instability began to mount in various regions.
- Criminal organizations from Latin America to Russia to Asia began to operate openly and often violently. It was increasingly difficult to distinguish between rebels and criminals. Meanwhile, the US recession deepened and American voters became more isolationist, especially as terrorist attacks on US soil increased.
- As the US recession continued and the American public became insecure and lethargic, the federal budget went into serious deficit spending to improve the social safety net and to create jobs. The military budget, already about 60 percent

of its earlier (2005) figure, no longer kept pace` with annual inflation.

In terms of a world "heavily influenced by the memories of terrorism, war, and instability that followed US isolationism":

- Slightly more than a year after the *Proteus: Insights from 2020* was published, on the morning of September 11, 2001, while this principal author was having discussion in his office with high-level US delegates from the CIA and NRO among others, his secretary in a great panic rushed in to inform him of the attack on the twin towers in New York. The US delegation included senior leadership that needed to know about major events affecting US national security, and yet they were all dumbfounded.

Obama /Hilary

In terms of terrible US foreign policy blunders subsequent to 2000, this principal author believes the worst could only be then-President George W. Bush's disastrous decision to invade Iraq.

In June 2001, this principal author was shocked to hear President Bush's appraisal of Russian President Vladimir Putin:

I looked the man in the eye. I found him to be very straightforward and trustworthy. And we had a very good dialogue. I was able to get a sense of his soul. He's a man deeply committed to his country and the best interests of his country. And I appreciated very much the frank dialogue. There was no kind of diplomatic chitchat, trying to throw each other off balance. There was a straightforward dialogue, and that's the beginning of a very constructive relationship.[26]

---

[26] 2001 June 18, "Transcript: Bush, Putin news conference," http://www.cnn.com/2001/WORLD/europe/06/18/bush.putin.transcript/index.html and
   User-created clip, 2014 March 3, "Bush Trusts Putin," https://www.c-span.org/video/?c4485932/bush-trusts-putin

Putin's Black Belt Judo Strategy

Sadly for America and the entire free world, just slightly more than one year earlier, President Bush had specifically been alerted to the prowess of Putin, who had just been inaugurated as the new president of Russia in May 2000. At the moment when *Proteus: Insights from 2020* was just being officially released, this principal author as Canada's then-Head and Thrust leader of Defence Space Systems and Technology, in charge of all Canadian defence R&D related to surveillance from space, surveillance of space, ballistic missile defence and nuclear radiation, was at a bilateral US-Canada discussion involving senior leaders of the US intelligence community. One of the US senior leaders, the then-Director of CIA, George J. Tenet arrived late and apologized profusely for his late arrival to such a high-level bilateral national meeting. He indicated that he had to go to the White House to specifically caution the president to be careful with President Putin. Putin was an officer in the KGB (the Soviet Union's intelligence service) and was appointed by Boris Yeltsin as the director of the FSB (Federal Security Service, which along with the SVR (Foreign Intelligence Service) succeeded the former KGB. Putin has a black belt in judo. In judo, a physically smaller practitioner can bring down a much stronger opponent by getting into a highly-stable position and carefully observing his opponent in order to identify and exploit the opponent's weaknesses and instability, thereby bringing the opponent down.

Interestingly enough, Tod Robberson's opinion piece in the *Dallas News* speculated: "I think Bush's own CIA and FBI specialists would have told him to read his intelligence briefs more closely before opening his mouth."[27]

Putin has not been shy in advertising the link between judo technique and political manoeuvring. His official website states: "Judo teaches self-control, the ability to feel the moment, to see the opponent's strengths

---

[27] Tod Robberson, 2010 June, "I looked the man (Putin) in the eye and saw ... the enemy," https://dallasnews.com/opinion/opinion/2010/06/29/i-looked-the-ma

and weaknesses, to strive for the best results. I am sure you will agree that these are essential abilities and skills for any politician."[28]

It was an enormous tragedy for the US that Bush did not appreciate the direct brief he received on Putin's tactical prowess. In hindsight, considering what Putin has done since then, the *Dallas News* hit the nail on the head with their June 2010 column titled, "I looked the man (Putin) in the eye and saw … the enemy."[29]

Much attention has been paid to the likelihood that Russian elements, under Putin's leadership, attempted to influence the US presidential election of 2016. But few if any political pundits or investigative journalists have raised the possibility of Russian efforts to influence then-President Bush to attack Iraq in 2003.

In view of Putin's pride in applying judo strategy as a politician, one could imagine him manoeuvring—perhaps manipulating Bush—during their "very good dialogue" in June 2001. Perhaps he suspected that Bush regarded then-president of Iraq Saddam Hussein as exemplifying the crux of Middle Eastern problems. Putin could have condoned or even affirmed Bush's focus on Iraq, reducing the US's attention on Russia while nudging the US into the debacle in Iraq.

In June 2004, CNN reported President Putin's claim that "Russian intelligence services warned Washington several times that Saddam Hussein's regime planned terrorist attacks against the United States:"[30]

> The warnings were provided after September 11, 2001 and before the start of the Iraqi war, Putin said….
>
> The planned attacks were targeted both inside and outside the United States, said Putin….

---

[28] Vladimir Putin's personal website, "Interests: Sport," http://en.putin.kremlin.ru/interests

[29] Tod Robberson, 2010 June, "I looked the man (Putin) in the eye and saw … the enemy," https://dallasnews.com/opinion/opinion/2010/06/29/i-looked-the-ma

[30] CNN, 2004 June 18, "Russia 'warned US about Saddam," http://www.cnn.com/2004/WORLD/europe/06/18/russia.warning/

He said the information was given to US intelligence officers and that US President George W. Bush expressed his gratitude to a top Russian intelligence official.

It is worth examining the true nature of the perceived 'help' the US received from Russia before invading Iraq. The *Washington Post*[31] also reported Putin's claims:

> After Sept. 11, 2001, and before the start of the military operation in Iraq, the Russian special services, the intelligence service, received information that officials from Saddam's regime were preparing terrorist attacks in the United States and outside it against the US military and other interests.

Both the CNN and the *Washington Post* reported that George Bush "had an opportunity to personally thank the head [or leader] of one of the Russian special services for this information, which he regarded as very important."

In contrast to Bush's alleged gratitude to Russia, the *Washington Post* article continued:

> A senior US intelligence official said yesterday that Russia has provided helpful information in the war on terrorism, but that he was "not aware of any specific threat information we were told" about Iraqi activities before the March 2003 invasion.

It is possible that Bush was grateful to Putin for 'helpfully' warning him of Saddam Hussein's planned attack, thereby lending crucial support to his decision to decisively attack Iraq. Yet the US intelligence community denied the usefulness of Russia's threat information.

---

[31] Walter Pincus, 2004 June 19, "Russia Warned US About Iraq, Putin Says," http://www.washingtonpost.com/wp-dyn/articles/A53096-2004Jun18.html

Russia's warning could have been part of Putin's conspiracy to bolster Bush's conviction that Iraq posed a severe threat.

Bearing in mind that the Soviets had experienced firsthand the damaging legacy of a unilateral, lengthy, and bloody invasion in Afghanistan, then if there is a grain of truth to the above speculation, President Bush's decision to attack Iraq would have been a momentous prize for Putin. Putin would have used his judo strategy to advance the ultimate goal of getting the Yankees to Go Home. Without marching into Iraq, the US could have saved an enormous amount of money and more importantly saved on the priceless life of US and Allied soldiers. If Putin intentionally played a role in nudging Bush toward that fateful choice, it would have been a striking feat with a much more severe impact on the wellbeing of the US as a nation than any Russian influence over the 2016 presidential election.

Bush's presidency came to an end in 2008 when Barack Obama's election victory made him the first African-American president of the US. Shortly before his November 2012 reelection, in August 2012 President Obama famously drew a "red line"[32] against the Syrian regime's use of chemical weapons, only to shy away from meting out consequences. Obama's bluff was just one episode in the continuing saga of the US's diminishing credibility and dependability as a global power.

Then-Secretary of Defense Chuck Hagel shared: "I think it did hurt the credibility of the president of the United States," and

When a president of the United States says something, especially about foreign policy or about another leader of another country, that means something, and we have to understand that that means something, and the president and the White House has to understand that means something.[33]

---

[32] Office of the Press Secretary, 2012 August 20, "Remarks by the President to the White House Press Corps," https://obamawhitehouse.archives.gov/the-press-office/2012/08/20/remarks-president-white-house-press-corps

[33] David Smith, 2016 January 14, "Former US defense chief: Obama 'hurt credibility'

This has helped to pave the way for significant opportunities for Putin to step into geopolitical power vacuums in Europe and the Middle East.

'Putin Plays Our Presidents for Fools' Bombshells

Ron Fournier of the *National Journal* wrote on March 2, 2014 an article entitled: "Why Putin Plays Our Presidents for Fools." [34] The subtitle was: "I looked into his eyes once, and what I saw scared me half to death." Fournier observed:

> The United States was caught off guard and impotent on Georgia, and again with regard to Ukraine, because of a fundamental misunderstanding of the cynicism and pragmatism that motivates Putin.... Putin exploited it to satiate his (and his country's) appetite for new territory and power.

Fournier concluded by lamenting:

> It is very sad indeed that both Bush and Obama have failed to realize that Putin, a former KGB officer, does not think like them and does not act in accordance with Western rules and customs, and ... a retrenched United States creates a leadership vacuum that they can fill, brutally.

---

by not bombing Syria in 2013," https://www.theguardian.com/us-news/2016/jan/14/chuck-hagel-barack-obama-hurt-credibility-pledge-bomb-syria-chemical-weapons referring to 2016 January 13, "Reflections of a Former Secretary of Defense," http://www.atlanticcouncil.org/events/webcasts/reflections-of-a-former-secretary-of-defense

[34] Ron Fournier, 2014 March 2, "Why Putin Plays Our Presidents for Fools," https://www.theatlantic.com/politics/archive/2014/03/why-putin-plays-our-presidents-for-fools/461055/

Trump's Bombshell Ascent to the US Presidency

In 2016, Donald J. Trump's election victory stunned the world. In March 2017, soon after Trump assumed the presidency, Politico's Europe edition expressed serious European concern about Putin and "Russia's plot against the West."[35] The article highlighted:

> The Kremlin wants to destroy the trans-Atlantic alliance....
>
> Moscow seeks nothing less than a reversal of the momentous historical processes begun in 1989, when Central and Eastern Europeans peacefully reclaimed their freedom.... Putin is implacably hostile to the United States, blaming it for bringing down the Soviet empire and humiliating Russia. Because the European Union and NATO ... serve as obstacles to the reassertion of Russian hegemony, Moscow's long-term strategy is to undermine and ultimately break these institutions from within.... The Kremlin's ideal outcome is the "Finlandization" of the West, whereby Europe and America abandon their principles, sacrifice their allies, and accommodate Kremlin prerogatives.

To the disappointment of many Western political leaders, ever since ascending to the White House, Trump has shown protectionist, isolationist, and abdicationist tendencies. In an opinion piece published in April 2018 by *The New York Times*,[36] former Secretary of State Madeleine Albright decried what she deemed was President Trump's isolationist approach to international affairs and failure to curb the spread of despotism around the world. Albright warned of the growing threat of a resurgence of fascism and criticized Trump for withdrawing the US from the global leadership role that has helped maintain international order.

---

[35] James Kirchick, 2017 March 17, "Russia's plot against the West," https://www.politico.eu/article/russia-plot-against-the-west-vladimir-putin-donald-trump-europe/

[36] Madeleine Albright, 2018 April 6, "Will We Stop Trump Before It's Too Late?" https://www.nytimes.com/2018/04/06/opinion/sunday/trump-fascism-madeleine-albright.html

In December 2017, Richard Haass, the president of the Council on Foreign Relations, wrote in *The Atlantic* an article called "America and the Great Abdication."[37] He remarked:

> Trump is the first post–World War II American president to view the burdens of world leadership as outweighing the benefits.... This change has major implications. It will make it far more difficult to deal with the challenges posed by globalization, including climate change and nuclear proliferation, to regulate cyberspace on terms compatible with American interests, or to help relieve the plight of refugees on terms consistent with American values. It will make it more difficult to build frameworks that promote trade and investment and to ensure that the United States benefits from.

Trump Is No More Isolationist than Obama Was

In November 2017, David Rosenberg argued in the Israeli newspaper *Haaretz* that "Trump Isn't Any More an Isolationist Than Obama Was."[38] Rosenberg opined:

America may be surrendering global leadership, but it was doing that long before Trump was handed the keys to the White House. Just note the Obama administration's unwillingness to entangle the US in Syria, Libya, Ukraine or other global flashpoints. George Bush, America seemed to overreach in foreign policy, fighting seemingly endless and far-off wars in Afghanistan and Iraq, which aroused anxieties that are

---

37 Richard Haass, 2017 December 28, "America and the Great Abdication," https://www.theatlantic.com/international/archive/2017/12/america-abidcation-trump-foreign-policy/549296/

38 David Rosenberg, 2017 November 15, "Trump Isn't Any More an Isolationist Than Obama Was," https://www.haaretz.com/world-news/.premium-trump-isnt-any-more-an-isolationist-than-obama-was-1.5465505

shared across the US political spectrum. So it was a natural that the next administration would withdraw.

Trump's Bombshell Decisions

Setting aside Trump's various idiosyncrasies, since taking office he has made daring decisions such as:

1. in December 2017 recognizing Jerusalem as the capital of Israel, reversing nearly seven decades of US foreign policy and marking a major milestone for Israel's claims over Jerusalem, which the international community has refrained from recognizing pending further negotiations with the Palestinians;

2. agreeing in March 2018 to meet with North Korean leader Kim Jong Un,[39] setting the stage for an unprecedented encounter between two nations that had only weeks earlier threatened to wipe each other out;[40] and

3. decertifying the nuclear deal with Iran in October 2017, followed by declaring in May 2018 that the US was withdrawing from the agreement, undoing his predecessor's foreign policy achievement.[41]

---

[39] 2018 March 8, "Remarks by Republic of Korea National Security Advisor Chung Eui-Yong," https://www.whitehouse.gov/briefings-statements/remarks-republic-korea-national-security-advisor-chung-eui-yong/

[40] Jeremy Diamond and Euan McKirdy, 2018 March 9, "Trump accepts offer to meet Kim Jong Un," https://www.cnn.com/2018/03/08/politics/donald-trump-kim-jong-un/index.html and

CBS/Associated Press, 2018 January 1, "Kim Jong Un warns "button for nuclear weapons is on my table"" https://www.cbsnews.com/news/kim-jong-un-north-korea-completed-nuclear-forces/ and

Jim Sciutto and Dana Bash, 2018 March 1, "Nuclear missile threat a 'red line' for Trump on North Korea," https://www.cnn.com/2018/03/01/politics/north-korea-trump-nuclear-missile-threat-red-line/index.html

[41] Mark Landler, 2018 May 8, "Trump Abandons Iran Nuclear Deal He Long Scorned," https://www.nytimes.com/2018/05/08/world/middleeast/trump-iran-nuclear-deal.html

In May 2018, Bret Stephens, reputedly a loud critic of Trump, hailed the latter move in a *New York Times* piece titled "A Courageous Trump Call on a Lousy Iran Deal."[42]

Viewed from any point on the political spectrum, such courageous decisions have increased the US's influence in global geopolitics.

Bible Coming to Life Bombshells

Trump's various bombshell decisions related to Israel and Iran have prompted thoughts of the end times.

For example, in January 2018 the *Jerusalem Post* reported that a "prominent Christian author" (Bill Koenig) said the Bible was 'coming to life.' Koenig said on the radio: "We are living in the most significant and important time in Bible-prophecy history ..." and "The Bible is playing out right before our eyes."[43]

In May 2018, the Bible-news website *Breaking Israel News* had an article entitled "In Convergence of Prophecy and Politics, President Trump Withdraws from Iran Deal."[44] The article described the political Gordian Knot[45]—contrasting, for example, the varying degrees of dismay coming from Iranian, British, German, and French leadership; with Israeli Prime Minister Netanyahu's praise for Trump's "courageous leadership" in making a "historic move." The article pointed to the relative clarity offered by Rabbi Pinchas Winston, an end-of-days expert:

---

[42] Bret Stephens, 2018 May 8, "A Courageous Trump Call on a Lousy Iran Deal," https://www.nytimes.com/2018/05/08/opinion/trump-courageous-iran-decision.html

[43] Benjamin Glatt, 2018 January 8, "The Bible Is 'Coming to Life,' Prominent Christian Author Says," https://www.jpost.com/CHRISTIAN-NEWS/THE-BIBLE-IS-COMING-TO-LIFE-PROMINENT-CHRISTIAN-AUTHOR-SAYS-533119

[44] Adam Eliyahu Berkowitz, 2018 May 9, "In Convergence of Prophecy and Politics, President Trump Withdraws from Iran Deal," https://www.breakingisraelnews.com/107375/in-convergence-of-prophecy-and-politics-president-trump-withdraws-from-iran-deal/

[45] That is, a knot virtually impossible to disentangle

Rabbi Winston said, "It is no coincidence that Trump withdrew from the Iran deal at the same time Iran is confronting Israel in Syria.... The embassy is political and not part of the Temple but it is clearly a step in the process. On a political level, it is entirely incongruous but in a geula context, it makes total sense."

The article also cited the high praise given by the Sanhedrin, an initiative to reinstate the seventy-one elders in a Biblically mandated high court:

> "His [Trump's] withdrawal from the counsel of the evil nations reinforces our belief that Trump is following in the footsteps of the Persian King Cyrus who ended the Babylonian exile and helped the Jews build the Second Temple."

Can the US-Europe Alliance Survive Trump?

As part of what might take place after this, Trump's bombshell decision to withdraw from the Iran nuclear agreement has created perhaps the most severe discord between the US and its European allies since the end of World War II. In May 2018 after Trump withdrew from the agreement, German Chancellor Angela Merkel said: "Europe must take its destiny in its own hands; that's the task of the future."[46]

Newsweek observed that this was not Merkel's first such statement:

> Merkel made a similar appeal a year ago [in May 2017], following visits by President Donald Trump to her country and the NATO alliance in neighboring Belgium. The chancellor hinted that Trump's "America first" slogan and his frequent clashes

---

46 Euractive with Agence France Presse, 2018 May 11, "Merkel: Europe can no longer rely on US to 'protect' it," https://www.euractiv.com/section/future-eu/news/merkel-europe-can-no-longer-rely-on-us-to-protect-it/

with US allies across the Atlantic were indicative of a wider schism in the Western alliance."[47]

World leaders continued to react in May 2018. The British newspaper *The Independent* reported: "The president of the European Council [Donald Tusk] has torn into Donald Trump, warning that the US president is a bad friend who acts with 'capricious assertiveness.'"[48] Tusk reportedly said:

- he was "grateful" for Trump because he had "made us realise that if you need a helping hand, you will find one at the end of your arm;" and
- Europe must be prepared to go it alone in some circumstances, because the shift in US politics under Trump's administration has made the US "an unreliable ally."

At the same time, *Foreign Policy* magazine posed the question: "Can the US-Europe Alliance Survive Trump?"[49] The ensuing article observed: "Europe and the United States have quarreled before. This time, it's serious." According to a former deputy national security advisor to US Vice President Joe Biden, European allies are feeling betrayed and angry, with some of them "already issuing last rites on the relationship."

---

[47] Damien Sharkov, 2018 May 11, "Angela Merkel: Europe Can No Longer Rely on US Protection," http://www.newsweek.com/europe-cannot-fully-rely-us-protection-anymore-says-germanys-merkel-919410 referring to 2017 May 28, "Merkel: Europe 'can no longer rely on allies' after Trump and Brexit," retrieved from http://www.bbc.com/news/world-europe-40078183

[48] Jon Stone, 2018 May 16, "EU president tears into Donald Trump, warning US president is bad friend who acts with 'capricious assertiveness'," https://www.independent.co.uk/news/uk/politics/eu-president-donald-trump-tusk-steel-tariff-iran-nuclear-deal-trade-sofia-western-balkans-a8354171.html

[49] Keith Johnson, Dan de Luce, Emily Tamkin, 2018 May 18, "Can the US-Europe Alliance Survive Trump?" foreignpolicy.com/2018/05/18/can-the-u-s-europe-alliance-survive-trump/

Soon after, in June 2018 at the forty-fourth G7 summit, Trump showed willingness to abandon the G7 and even aim the wrecking ball against the pillars of 'the West.'[50] An author from the Council of Foreign Relations wrote:

"Sobering and a bit depressing." That was German Chancellor Angela Merkel's verdict of Donald J. Trump's latest temper tantrum.

He is destined to be one of America's most consequential foreign policy presidents. Fewer than seventeen months into his administration, Trump has already shaken the foundations of international order. He has abdicated US global leadership, which he believes has bled the United States dry, and he has sidelined multilateral institutions (from NATO to the WTO), which he perceives constrain US freedom of action. He seems prepared to abandon ... the concept of "the West" as pillars of US global engagement.

The following month, in July 2018, Politico's Europe Edition described a two-day NATO summit as a case of "whiplash" caused by Trump's inconsistent messaging:

> Donald Trump unleashed havoc at NATO on Thursday [July 12, 2018], threatening to pull out if America's allies don't boost military spending then praising the alliance as a "fine-tuned machine."
>
> The president disoriented NATO leaders for the entire two-day meeting, with a whiplash performance that included chiding Germany and delivering what one official called a "prolonged rant" on spending. It fits into his defined pattern of creating chaos at major summits, such as his blow-up at a G7 summit in Quebec.

---

[50]   Stewart M. Patrick, 2018 June 11, "At G7 Summit, Trump Takes a Wrecking Ball to the West," https://www.cfr.org/blog/g7-summit-trump-takes-wrecking-ball-west

Similarly, *USA Today* reported:

> "In Brussels, he berated NATO allies over their defense spend-
> ing, even privately threatening to walk out of the alliance—only
> to sign on to a unanimous declaration acknowledging the alli-
> ance has made progress. By the end, he declared NATO "much
> stronger than it was two days ago."[51]

Also in July 2018, *The Atlantic* published a blunt headline: "The Self-
Inflicted Demise of American Power: The effect of Trump's foreign-policy
doctrine can be summed up as 'Make America Weak Again.'"[52] The
Atlantic opined:

> America's preeminence on the world stage rests on five essen-
> tial sources of power: neighbors, allies, markets, values, and
> military might. The Trump Doctrine is weakening all of them
> except the military.

The article concluded:

> The effect of the Trump Doctrine is Making America Weak Again
> by diminishing the role of American values, and with them our
> standing in the world.
>   International-relations scholars have long found that great
> powers typically fall for two reasons: imperial overstretch or
> rivalry with other great powers. Never in world history has a
> country declined because of so many self-inflicted attacks on
> the sources of its own power.

---

[51] Gregory Korte, 2018 July 12, Trump's chaotic NATO summit raises stakes for Putin talks in Helsinki, https://www.usatoday.com/story/news/politics/2018/07/12/trump-nato-summit-putin-talks-helsinki/779598002/

[52] Amy Zegart, 2018 July 12, "The Self-Inflicted Demise of American Power," https://www.theatlantic.com/international/archive/2018/07/trump-nato-summit/565034/

Trump-Putin Summit

Conversely, Trump's closeness with Russian President Putin has provoked concern. In July 2018, the two presidents held a joint press conference in Helsinki, Finland. Trump's performance was puzzling. News outlets including *The Economist* reported on Donald Trump's humiliation in Helsinki:[53]

> In Helsinki, asked whether Russia had attacked America's democracy, he treated President Vladimir Putin as someone he trusts more than his own intelligence agencies. It was a rotten result for America and the world.
>
> Americans were more than usually outraged. At the post-summit press conference in Helsinki, with the world watching and the American flag behind him, their head of state had appeared weak (see article). He was unwilling to stand up for America in the face of an assault that had been graphically described three days earlier by Robert Mueller, the special counsel probing election meddling, in his indictment of twelve Russian military-intelligence officers.

Likewise, the *New York Times* and CNN declared Putin's "win" in face of Trump's humiliation.[54]

---

[53] See for example *The Economist*, 2018 July 21, "Donald Trump's humiliation in Helsinki," https://www.economist.com/leaders/2018/07/21/donald-trumps-humiliation-in-helsinki

And *San Francisco Chronicle*, "Editorial: Trump-Putin summit—an American humiliation,"https://www.sfchronicle.com/opinion/editorials/article/Editorial-Trump-Putin-summit-an-American-13079259.php

And *The Globe and Mail* (Canada), 2018 July 16, "Globe editorial: Donald Trump humiliated himself and his country in Helsinki," https://www.theglobeandmail.com/opinion/editorials/article-globe-editorial-donald-trump-humiliated-himself-and-his-country-in/

[54] Elena Chernenko, 2018 July 16, "An Easy Win for Vladimir Putin," https://www.nytimes.com/2018/07/16/opinion/putin-trump-meeting-helsinki.html

And Stephen Collinson, updated 2018 July 18, "Discord over Trump's Helsinki

Stateside the following day, Trump attempted to reverse course by claiming that he misspoke about Russia's interference in the 2016 US presidential election. Trump claimed that he meant to say "I don't see any reason why it wouldn't be Russia" instead of his humiliating statement that he saw no reason why it "would" be Russia. Neither accepting nor questioning Trump's explanation, the *New York Times* put it to their readers to assess Trump's true beliefs about Russia:[55]

> Here is what he said Monday, without notes, as he stood beside the Russian leader, Vladimir Putin, on that and other subjects.
> We invite you to read the president's own words and decide for yourself what he really thinks.

For this principal author, it appears that President Trump is not entirely convinced of Putin's effort to undermine the US. Just like former president George W. Bush, not even a direct briefing from the Director of CIA has enabled Trump to perceive the reality that this covert black belt judo practitioner is an enemy to the US including its democratic and judicial systems. Not only should investigations continue into Putin's possible efforts to interfere with the 2016 US presidential election, but probes should also extend to Putin's possible influence in persuading then-president Bush to launch the disastrous Iraq invasion of 2003.

As noted above, in 2014 the *National Journal*'s Ron Fournier wrote about "Why Putin Plays Our Presidents for Fools." Surely we could add Trump's name to the list of US presidents being played for fools.

---

humiliation hands Putin another win," https://www.cnn.com/2018/07/18/politics/donald-trump-vladimir-putin-finland-summit-fallout/index.html

[55] See for example New York Times Editorial Board, 2018 July 17, Trump Says He Got Only One Word Wrong. Please Decide for Yourself. https://www.nytimes.com/interactive/2018/07/17/opinion/editorials/trump-putin-helsinki-summit-editorial.html

The US Withdrawal from the Middle East and Europe

In December 2018, CNN reported: "Trump orders rapid withdrawal from Syria in apparent reversal:"[56]

> President Donald Trump has ordered staff to execute the "full" and "rapid" withdrawal of US military from Syria, declaring that the US has defeated ISIS.
>
> "We have defeated ISIS in Syria, my only reason for being there during the Trump Presidency," Trump tweeted Wednesday morning. Planning for the pullout is already underway, a US defense official and an administration official told CNN.
>
> The decision, a sharp reversal from previously stated US policy, surprised foreign allies and lawmakers, sparking rebukes, rebuttals and warnings of intensified congressional oversight, even as the White House said troops are already on their way home.

Shortly after, CNN reported: "US military ordered to begin planning to withdraw about half the troops in Afghanistan."[57] The article highlighted:

> Gen. John Allen, a former commander of NATO and US forces in Afghanistan, told CNN on Thursday that a drawdown in Afghanistan would be a mistake.
>
> "Pulling out right now, just the announcement would create chaos in the strategy," Allen said.
>
> The US has about 14,000 troops in Afghanistan, most of which are present as part of a larger NATO-led mission to train, advise and assist Afghan forces. Any withdrawal would be

---

56 https://www.cnn.com/2018/12/19/politics/us-syria-withdrawal/index.html

57 **https://www.cnn.com/2018/12/20/politics/afghanistan-withdrawal/index.html**

complicated by the fact that the United States is part of NATO's Resolute Support mission.

Trump has long been critical of the US presence in Afghanistan, which began after the September 11, 2001, terrorist attacks. But lawmakers have echoed Allen's concern about a hasty departure.

Also in December 2018, the New York Times reported: "Defending Syria Withdrawal, Trump Says U.S. Should Not Be 'Policeman of the Middle East.'[58]"

The next day, CNN bluntly commented on "America's unprecedented 72 hours that could reshape the world,"[59] stating:

This is a "do not adjust your set" moment, in which the world's preeminent military power effectively withdrew from its two active battlefields, ceded the ground to its geopolitical rivals, and abandoned allies.

It is unprecedented. ...Trump's announcements about Syria and Afghanistan change something permanently. ...it is the message that is the most potent: the casual disregard of history, ally, or duty.

It says the Commander in Chief considers his own gut paramount, and the decades of sacrifice that got America to this point of lesser importance.

Later in December 2018, Trump made a surprise visit to Iraq, and it was immediately reported across the world in headlines such as " Trump declares end to US 'policeman' role in surprise Iraq visit."[60]

---

58 https://www.nytimes.com/2018/12/20/us/politics/trump-syria-withdrawal.html

59 https://www.cnn.com/2018/12/21/politics/trump-syria-afghanistan-us-military/index.html

60 Gulf Times, https://www.gulf-times.com/story/617631/Trump-declares-end-to-US-policeman-role-in-surpris

Very sadly, it seems Trump has followed exactly the predictive script laid out in *Proteus: Insights from 2020* on Yankee Going Home Scenario such as:

- US armed forces and their equipment being brought home;
- the 'police' everyone had taken for granted going home.

Though there might be some delays in pulling out US troops from Syria and Afghanistan, Trump as a President with strong business experience is fully aware that the US can no longer afford to play the role of policeman for the entire world, especially with ever more challenges to contain the spread of terrorism and nuclearization around the world.

Trump's seemingly endless bombshells would not only reshape the geopolitical landscape of the Middle East but might prove to be a significant turning point leading the US to eventually withdraw from the European political arena. That in turn would make way for a ten-king coalition with little US involvement.[61] This will be further discussed in Chapter 8 of this book.

The NRO's Yankee Going Home forecast—in terms of the US's retreat from the Middle East and eventually Europe—are fully in line with the Bible's prophetic silence regarding the US's role in end times.

In the wake of Trump's various bombshell decisions, Iran is likely to play a much more significant role in the Middle East in conjunction with Russia. Chapters 3 and 5 of this book expand on this line of thinking as another part of What Might Take Place After This.

Proverbs 21:1 states: "The king's heart is in the hand of the LORD, as the rivers of water: he turneth it whithersoever he will" (King James Version). Since the "king's heart" is in God's hand, the question arises: why does God appear to limit America's role in end-time geopolitics?

The Bible's statements regarding end-time geopolitics specifically refer to a power from the North, Persia, Cush, Put (Libya) (Daniel 11),

---

[61] Daniel chapter 7 describes Daniel's vision of a ten-horned beast representing ten nations

and an army of 200 million from the east (Revelation 16:12 and 9:16), but nothing of substance about the US.

Why would God disallow the US from retaining its mighty influence after it had risen to the heights of a lonely superpower and dominated the world scene for much of the twentieth century?

In a related vein, two days after the September 11, 2001 attack, Billy Graham's daughter was asked, "How could God let something like this happen?" Anne Graham gave a profound and insightful response, saying:

> I say God is also angry when he sees something like this. I would say also for several years now Americans in a sense have shaken their fist at God and said, God, we want you out of our schools, our government, our business, we want you out of our market-place. And God, who is a gentleman, has just quietly backed out of our national and political life, our public life. Removing his hand of blessing and protection."[62]

Going back to basics, "In God We Trust," carried on US bank notes and coins was meant as a daily reminder to all Americans that: "No nation can be strong except in the strength of God, or safe except in His defense. The trust of our people in God should be declared."[63]

My Glory Will I Not Give to Graven Images

Many if not most US presidents have claimed to be Christians. It might come as a surprise that President Obama more clearly articulated his Christian beliefs than other presidents, professing for example that

---

[62] The Early Show, 2001 September 13, "Where Is God?," http://web.archive.org/web/20010913185312/http://www.cbsnews.com/earlyshow/healthwatch/healthnews/20010913terror_spiritual.shtml

[63] 19.https://www.treasury.gov/about/education/Pages/in-god-we-trust.aspx

We are no longer a christian nation — OBAMA

Christ "our Savior, who suffered and died was resurrected, both fully God and also a man."[64] Yet many Christians have criticized Obama and doubted his faith because he championed gay rights in the US and did not shy away from imposing sanctions on sovereign foreign governments that limited gay rights, such as the government in Uganda.

But the president is only one of the three branches of US government (the executive branch), the others being the legislative (Congress), and the judicial (courts). Back in 1962, the judicial branch (the US Supreme Court) already ruled that it is unconstitutional for schools to encourage students to recite an official school prayer in public schools.[65]

In March 2014, the US Congress invited the Dalai Lama to pray to Buddha in the opening prayer of the US Senate.[66] He was also invited to join the 2015 Annual National Prayer Breakfast.[67]

The US Congressional leadership would do well to consider Isaiah 42:8: "I am the Lord: that is my name: and my glory will I not give to another, neither my praise to graven images (KJV)."

Can the US Return Back to God?

Can the formerly-formidable US, as a nation, turn back to God?

Can it be done?

God has said in 2 Chronicles 7:14: "If my people, *ISRAEL* which are called by my name, shall humble themselves, and pray, and seek my face, and

---

[64] 20 Office of the Press Secretary, 2013 April 5, "Remarks by the President and Vice President at Easter Prayer Breakfast," https://obamawhitehouse.archives.gov/the-press-office/2013/04/05/remarks-president-and-vice-president-easter-prayer-breakfast

[65] *Engel v. Vitale*, 370 US 421 (1962)

[66] Alex Rogers, 2014 March 6, "Dalai Lama Gives Prayer on Senate Floor," http://time.com/14056/dalai-lama-senate-prayer/

[67] Elizabeth Dias, 2015 January 29, "Exclusive: Dalai Lama, Barack Obama Set to Appear in Public Together for First Time," http://time.com/3687508/dalai-lama-prayer-breakfast/

turn from their wicked ways; then will I hear from heaven, and will forgive their sin, and will heal their land" (KJV).

In July 2012, the last great evangelical crusader Billy Graham at age ninety-three, wrote:[68]

> Some years ago, my wife, Ruth, was reading the draft of a book I was writing … she startled me by exclaiming, "If God doesn't punish America, He'll have to apologize to Sodom and Gomorrah."
>
> My heart aches for America. The wonderful news is that our Lord is a God of mercy, and He responds to repentance. In Jonah's day, Nineveh was the lone world superpower—wealthy, unconcerned, and self-centered. When the Prophet Jonah finally traveled to Nineveh and proclaimed God's warning, people heard and repented.
>
> I believe the same thing can happen once again, this time in our nation.

In anticipation of Christ's return, the aching hearts of many US Christians and Christian leaders are yearning to 'make America turn back to God' rather than to 'make America great again.'

---

[68] Billy Graham, 2012 July 19, "My Heart Aches for America," https://billygraham.org/story/billy-graham-my-heart-aches-for-america/.

CHAPTER 3

THE UTTERMOST NORTH
BOMBSHELL

Gog and Magog

For at least two centuries, biblical scholars have wondered if Russia is related to the prophecies of Ezekiel regarding Gog, Magog, Mesheck, and Tubal.

The Bible tells us that Gog is the leader from the land of Magog (Ezekiel 38:2-3 and 39:1). Learned scholars are not absolutely clear where the land of Magog is except that it is situated in the "uttermost parts of the north" from Israel's point of view (Ezekiel 38:6 and 15; 39:2, ESV). Northward travel from Israel leads through Lebanon, Syria, Turkey, the Black Sea, and finally Russia all the way up to the Arctic Circle.

The Bible says that this great northern power is the leader of Tubal and Mesheck. Some connect these names to the modern Russian cities of Moscow (reminiscent of 'Meschech') and Tobolsk (reminiscent of 'Tubal'). The Scofield Study Bible states: "The reference to Meshech and Tubal (Moscow and Tobolsk) is a clear mark of identification."

US author Derek Walker writes:[69] "The name Moscow derives from

---

[69] Appendix 6 to *The Imminent Invasion of Israel*, retrieved from

CHRIST'S RETURN AND TODAY'S GLOBAL GEOPOLITICAL BOMBSHELLS

the tribal name Meshech, and Tobolsk, the name of the principal state, from Tubal.... L.Sale-Harrison corroborated this identification on linguistic grounds."

Ezekiel 38 and 39 foresee that Gog and Magog will align with other nations to form a formidable army against Israel. Ezekiel refers to Persia (modern-day Iran), Put (modern-day Libya), Cush (modern-day Sudan), Gomer (Turkey), and Beth Togamah (part of modern-day Turkey or possibly Syria). If the latter indeed refers to Turkey, that would be a remarkable addition to this line-up of nations joining the Gog-Magog alliance.

Turkey Bombshell

Turkey has been part of the North Atlantic Treaty Organization (NATO) since 1952 and has been eager to join the European Union. For decades it was almost unthinkable that it would join forces with Russia, which has been hostile to NATO. As of late, however, Turkey seems to be on a different trajectory.

Back in December 2016, a *Washington Post* columnist described "How the Obama administration pushed Turkey into Russia's arms."[70] He stated:

> Much of the Washington foreign policy community stood aghast Tuesday as top officials of NATO ally Turkey sat down with leaders of Russia and Iran in Moscow to forge a new way forward for Syria, without the United States in the room. The scene was not only a turning point in the Syrian crisis but also a stunning

---

https://www.oxfordbiblechurch.co.uk/index.php/books/the-imminent-invasion-of-israel/542-appendix-6-where-is-meshech-and-tubal

[70] Josh Rogin, 2016 December 22, "How the Obama administration pushed Turkey into Russia's arms," https://www.washingtonpost.com/news/josh-rogin/wp/2016/12/22/how-the-obama-administration-pushed-turkey-into-russias-arms/?noredirect=on&utm_term=.f7aba33b1f70

display of Turkey's shifting orientation towards Russia and away from America and the West.

In August 2018, *the New York Times* editorial board published their opinion of "Turkey's Downward Spiral."[71] They observed:

> Not long ago it would have seemed unthinkable to add Turkey to the list of countries—including North Korea, Iran, and Russia—that the United States had sanctioned for unscrupulous behavior. Turkey has a mutual defense treaty with Washington, ... and hosts American nuclear weapons at Incirlik air base, near its border with Syria.
>
> The current tension is a far cry from the camaraderie expressed at the NATO meeting last month, when Mr. Trump fist-bumped Mr. Erdogan.
>
> But Mr. Erdogan's increasingly authoritarian rule and the regional unrest caused by the Syrian conflict have tested this bond.

Similarly, Michael Rubin, a resident scholar at the American Enterprise Institute, opined in the *Washington Post*: "It's time for Turkey and NATO to go their separate ways:"[72]

> Thousands of Turks fought alongside American forces during the Korean War..... If the United States was the alliance's backbone, Turkey was its muscle: even today, it has more men under arms than France and Germany combined.

71 New York Times Editorial Board, 2018 August 10, "Turkey's Downward Spiral," https://www.nytimes.com/2018/08/10/opinion/turkey-united-states-trump-erdogan.html

72 Michael Rubin, 2018 August 16, "It's time for Turkey and NATO to go their separate ways," https://www.washingtonpost.com/news/democracy-post/wp/2018/08/16/its-time-for-turkey-and-nato-to-go-their-separate-ways/

But all that was before Erdogan.... Erdogan has made it clear that he aims to purchase Russian S-400 missiles, which ... might compromise NATO air-defense secrets to Russian engineers.

Indeed, the real danger to NATO is ... that it remains inside. Because NATO decisions are consensual, Turkey can play the proverbial Trojan Horse to filibuster any action when crisis looms.

Also in August 2018, CNN published the opinion of Fadi Hakura, a Turkey expert and associate fellow at Chatham House, a London-based policy institute, that "The West cannot afford losing Turkey to Russia and Iran."[73] Hakura cautioned: "The West will pay a heavy price for losing such an important country as an ally."

Whatever geopolitical bombshells drop next, over two millennia ago Ezekiel already suggested that Turkey would figure in the Gog-Magog alliance which would attack Israel.

Putin, Master of the Middle East Bombshell

Turning back to the matter of Russia: During the Cold War, successive leaders from Khrushchev to Andropov sought to exploit the Arab-Israeli conflict in order to increase Moscow's influence in the Middle East in opposition to the US. At the end of the Cold War, as the Soviet Union disintegrated, Russia lost its superpower status, making the fulfillment of Ezekiel's prophecy seem impossible.

Today, president of Russia Vladimir Putin has single-handedly pulled Russia out from the abyss of a failed state, styling himself as the new master of the Middle East.[74] He holds himself out as modern Russia's

---

[73] Fadi Hakura, 2018 August 14, "The West cannot afford losing Turkey to Russia and Iran," https://www.cnn.com/2018/08/14/opinions/west-losing-turkey-opinion-intl/index.html

[74] Henry Meyer and Donna Abu-Nasr, 2017 October 3, "Putin Is Filling the Middle East Power Vacuum," https://www.bloomberg.com/news/articles/2017-10-03/putin-is-now-mr-middle-east-a-job-no-one-ever-succeeds-at

greatest national hero and claimed reelection by earning (however controversially) 76 percent of the votes cast. Black-belt judoka Putin has not only helped to wound the US's legacy as a lonely superpower, but he has also put Russia back on the world stage; his invasion of Georgia, annexation of Crimea, and posturing in Syria are just some of his geopolitical manoeuvers to restore Russia's global influence.

In October 2017, Tyler Duren wrote for *Bloomberg News* that Putin is "the new master of the Middle East:"[75]

> The Israelis and Turks, the Egyptians and Jordanians – they're all beating a path to the Kremlin in the hope that Vladimir Putin, the new master of the Middle East, can secure their interests and fix their problems.
>
> Until very recently, Washington stood alone as the go-to destination for such leaders. Right now, American power in the region is perceptibly in retreat—testimony to the success of Russia's military intervention in Syria.
>
> "Putin has succeeded in making Russia a factor in the Middle East," said Dennis Ross, who advised several presidents from George H. W. Bush to Barack Obama.

Earlier in 2017, the Israeli newspaper *Haaretz* published an opinion piece titled "Putin Is the Middle East's New Boss."[76] The subtitle read: "Six years after the start of the Syrian civil war, an Assad victory now seems assured thanks to Russia's military intervention."

The article observed:

---

[75] Henry Meyer and Donna Abu-Nasr, 2017 October 3, "Putin Is Filling the Middle East Power Vacuum," https://www.bloomberg.com/news/articles/2017-10-03/putin-is-now-mr-middle-east-a-job-no-one-ever-succeeds-at

[76] Amos Harel, "Putin Is the Middle East's New Boss," 2017 retrieved from https://www.haaretz.com/israel-news/putin-is-the-middle-easts-new-boss-1.5450162

In late 2016, the regime chalked up its biggest achievement—the surrender of rebel groups in Aleppo.

The wave of refugees from the Middle East, along with several deadly terror attacks, changed the internal political situation in Europe, and indirectly influenced … the surprising result in the US presidential election.

Russia reemerged on the world scene and reimposed a dual-superpower international reality. Russia has demonstrated that it does not abandon its wards.

Along the same vein, on December 13, 2017 CBS News described "How Putin made himself a Middle East power broker:[77]

"When Russia launched a military campaign in Syria two years ago, President Vladimir Putin sought to save his ally from imminent collapse and break Russia's international isolation over a crisis in Ukraine.

He achieved that and more, emerging as a key stakeholder in the Middle East who has brokered deals with many of its key players—from Iran to Saudi Arabia to Turkey and Israel.

It's a regional footprint that comes with a degree of clout that even the Soviet Union, which depended on a handful of Arab allies, couldn't dream of during the Cold War era."

As Trump began his US presidency, Russian leader Putin has become even more successful in bolstering Russia's global image of strength and hurting the US. In July 2018 after Trump's humiliating performance beside Putin (discussed in Chapter 2), CNN reported: "Trump caved spectacularly to Putin. Here's what might happen next:"[78]

---

[77] https://www.cbsnews.com/news/russias-vladimir-putin-middle-east-united-states-donald-trump/

[78] Stephen Collinson, updated 2018 July 17, "Trump caved spectacularly to Putin.

The formative moment in Putin's life came when he watched the evisceration of the Soviet empire from his post in Dresden, East Germany, after the fall of the Berlin Wall in 1989.

That searing experience nurtured a fierce grievance against the United States, the victor in the Cold War, and a political career dedicated to the reversal of Moscow's humiliation.

US intelligence experts said Putin will take one message from Monday's events: that Trump is weak and there is no price to be paid for warping US democracy.

Courting Favor with Religious Groups

Turning to a different matter: Over the years, Putin has carried out a distinctive style of diplomacy among devotees of major religious groups.

1. Toward Muslims: in May 2016, Putin declared Russia to be a "reliable ally" to the "Islamic world";[79]
2. Toward Christians in Syria: in December 2017, Putin vowed that Russia would "help rebuild Christian churches in Syria and establish peace in historically Christian regions of the war-torn country."[80]
3. Towards Russian Orthodox Christians: in July 2014, Putin "suggested rebuilding inside the Kremlin two monasteries and a church that were torn down during the Soviet era."[81]

Here's what might happen next," https://www.cnn.com/2018/07/17/politics/president-trump-vladimir-putin-summit-history/index.html

[79] Damien Sharkov, "Putin Declares Russia an 'Ally' to Islamic World," 2016 retrieved from www.newsweek.com/putin-declares-russia-ally-islamic-world-464160

[80] Cristina Maza, "Putin Vows to Rebuild Christian Syria, Restoring Churches and Bringing Refugees Home" 2017 retrieved from www.newsweek.com/russia-putin-rebuild-christian-syria-churches-735539

[81] "Putin Wants Monasteries, Church Rebuilt in Kremlin" 2014 retrieved from https://themoscowtimes.com/news/putin-wants-monasteries-church-rebuilt-in-kremlin-37894

- Toward Christians in general: in June 2012 during his Middle East tour, Putin stopped to kneel and pray in the Church of the Holy Sepulchre in Jerusalem. He reportedly "met Father Superior Isidore and the Patriarch of Jerusalem Theofilos III who were both very happy to see him again. This is not the first time he has been there. As Putin himself admits this is one of his favorite places to visit."[82]

- Toward the Jews: during the same trip to Jerusalem in June 2012, Putin visited the Western Wall (Wailing Wall) and—upon hearing an Israeli bystander explain the importance of the Temple Mount and the Jewish Temple—responded: "That's exactly the reason I came here—to pray for the Temple to be built again."[83]

Cancellation of Iran Nuclear Deal Bombshell

As Putin continues a Middle East power play, Russia is increasingly likely to assume the role of leading mighty armies to descend upon the Holy Land—thereby fulfilling a Bible prophecy from over 2,600 years ago.

The Trump administration's withdrawal from the nuclear agreement with Iran[84] is likely to increase the strength of bonds among the Bible's prophetical Russian-Iranian coalition involving other Israel-hating nations.

Indeed, Israeli Prime Minister Benjamin Netanyahu had loudly denounced the agreement with Iran, accusing the latter of failing to

---

[82] Dmitry Sudakov, "Putin kneels and prays in Jerusalem" 2012 retrieved from www.pravdareport.com/russia/politics/27-06-2012/121498-putin_jerusalem-0/

[83] Adam Eliyahu Berkowitz, "Sanhedrin Asks Putin and Trump to Build Third Temple in Jerusalem," 2016 retrieved from www.breakingisraelnews.com/78372/bin-exclusive-sanhedrin-asks-putin-trump-build-third-temple-jerusalem/

[84] Further discussed in Chapter 7

honour the deal.[85] Trump siding with Israel could only add fuel to the fire in terms of Iran's hatred of Israel.

Unfortunately for Israel, after Trump's bombshell withdrawal from the Iran nuclear deal, Putin reportedly reached out to European leaders including German chancellor Angela Merkel and French president Emmanuel Macron, proposing a shared "strategic interest."[86]

As reported by the *Financial Times*, Trump's bombshell seems to be driving European leaders to seek rapprochement with Russia, moving them further away from supporting Israel. This will further enhance Putin's influence in Europe and the Middle East—in line with the Bible prophecy pointing to the rise of a power from the uttermost parts of the north.

Furthermore, Trump's unreserved support of Israel will not last indefinitely. Future US presidents might not be as supportive; even the previous president Obama was ice cold in supporting Israel during his eight-year presidency.

Other background factors include the US's limited resources and the worrisome discord between the US and its European allies in terms of their respective views on Israel.

As this book was being prepared for printing. Trump shocked the world in announcing the withdrawal of US troops from Syria and partially from Afghanistan, thus beginning the unprecedented withdrawal from the Middle East geopolitical theatre.

[85] See for example Oliver Holmes and Julian Borger, Nuclear deal: Netanyahu accuses Iran of cheating on agreement," 2018 April 30 retrieved from https://www.theguardian.com/world/2018/apr/30/netanyahu-accuses-iran-cheating-nuclear-deal

   John Irish, Rania El Gamal, Steve Holland, "Europe licks wounds as Saudi Arabia and Israel hail Trump on Iran," 2018 May 9, retrieved from https://www.reuters.com/article/us-iran-nuclear-diplomacy/europe-licks-wounds-as-saudi-arabia-and-israel-hail-trump-on-iran-idUSKBN1IA38C

[86] "Wary EU powers find common ground with Kremlin," 2018 May 18, https://www.ft.com/content/6b92c9c4-5a75-11e8-bdb7-f6677d2e1ce8

US Withdrawal from the Middle East Paving the Way for Gog-Magog Invasion

Further to the discussion in Chapter 2 on US withdrawal from Syria and Afghanistan, on 19 December 2018, USA Today reported that "Trump reversal on Syria policy means big gains for Iran."[87]

Along the same tone, NBC News reported that "Trump's withdrawal from Syria is victory for Iran and Russia, experts say."[88]

> The move provides "Iran with solid control over the entire arc of the Levant from Baghdad to Beirut," one expert said.

On 20 December 2018, CNN reported that "Trump is leaving the fight against ISIS (and influence in the Middle East) to Russia and Iran."[89]

CNBC commented that "Trump's sudden Syria pullout will embolden ISIS and Iran, allies warn."[90]

With the similar tone, the New York Times reported "Syria Pullout by U.S. Tilts Mideast Toward Iran and Russia, Isolating Israel."[91] This news report further indicated that:

> The American decision to withdraw from Syria has abruptly scrambled the geopolitics of the Middle East, clearing the way for Iran to expand its influence across the region, leaving Israel virtually alone to stop it.

---

87 https://www.usatoday.com/story/opinion/2018/12/19/donald-trump-ordering-troops-syria-iran-israel-iraq-hezbollah-column/2367883002/

88 https://www.nbcnews.com/storyline/isis-uncovered/trump-s-withdrawal-syria-victory-iran-russia-experts-say-n950111

89 https://www.cnn.com/2018/12/19/middleeast/trump-troops-syria-npw-analysis-intl/index.html

90 html https://www.cnbc.com/2018/12/20/trumps-sudden-syria-pullout-will-embolden-isis-and-iran-allies-warn

91 https://www.nytimes.com/2018/12/20/world/middleeast/syria-us-withdrawal-iran.html

The decision shows that even a relatively small move —
the United States has only about 2,000 troops in Syria — can
have far-reaching consequences in a complex war, leaving allies
struggling to cope and adversaries pleased and emboldened.

"Donald's right, and I agree with him," said President
Vladimir V. Putin of Russia, whose influence over Syria can only
grow more dominant as the United States exits.

On 21 December 2018, Washington Post lamnted that "U.S. troop
withdrawal from Syria is a dream come true for the Iranians."[92]

Without any doubt, Trump's decision to eventually pull US troops
out of Syria and Afghanistan will be one of the most decisive bombshells
to geopolitically clear the way for Russia and Iran to start contemplating
their Gog-Magog raid of the Holy Land as prophesied 2.6 millennia ago
by the Bible.

Israel, the Land of Great Spoils

What might take place after this? The Bible tells us that Israel's friends
or allies will only be able to clamour in protest. Ezekiel 38:13 states:

> Sheba, and Dedan, and the merchants of Tarshish, with all the
> young lions thereof, shall say unto thee, Art thou come to take a
> spoil? hast thou gathered thy company to take a prey? to carry
> away silver and gold, to take away cattle and goods, to take a
> great spoil? (KJV)

What might take place after this? The foregoing Bible verse tells us
the reason why Russia and its allies would want to invade the Holy Land.

---

92 https://www.washingtonpost.com/world/us-troop-withdrawal-from-syria-is-a-
dream-come-true-for-the-iranians/2018/12/21/472b316a-04b2-11e9-958c-0a6012
26ff6b_story.html?utm_term=.cb7e8f17e2f9

So what prey and spoil does Israel possess, which would entice Russia to come to the Holy Land with such a large coalition of armies?

Some learned scholars have explored the possibility that King Solomon buried gold and treasure in some as-yet undiscovered area of the Holy Land. While that line of work presses on, prey and spoil might be found in Israeli "black gold."

In June 1973, the *New York Times* reported a wry lament by then-premier of Israel Golda Meir, during a state dinner for West German chancellor Willy Brandt: "Let me tell you something that we Israelis have against Moses; he took us forty years through the desert in order to bring us to the one spot in the Middle East that has no oil."[93]

Contrary to Golda Meir's remark, in recent years the Holy Land has proven to be not only a land of milk and honey but also a land of plentiful gas and oil.

In October 2015, Fox News reported the discovery of "potentially game-changing oil reserves" in Israel:[94]

> Afek Oil and Gas, an Israeli subsidiary of the US company Genie Energy, confirmed the find in an interview with Israel's Channel 2 TV.... "We are talking about a strata which is 350 meters thick and what is important is the thickness and the porosity," the company's chief geologist, Yuval Bartov, explained. "On average in the world, strata are 20-30 meters thick, so this is ten times as large as that, so we are talking about significant quantities. The

---

[93] "Mrs. Meir Says Moses Made Israel Oil-Poor," 1973 June 11, page 3 of the *New York Times*

[94] Simon Tomlinson, "Discovery of oil in ISRAEL means the Jewish state could soon produce 'significant quantities' of 'black gold' and potentially change the face of the Middle East," 2015 October 8, retrieved from http://www.dailymail.co.uk/news/article-3265023/Discovery-oil-ISRAEL-means-Jewish-state-soon-produce-significant-quantities-black-gold-potentially-change-face-Middle-East.html

Paul Alster, "Potentially game-changing oil reserves discovered in Israel," 2015 October 8, retrieved from http://www.foxnews.com/world/2015/10/07/potentially-game-changing-oil-reserves-discovered-in-israel.html

important thing is to know the oil is in the rock and that's what we now know."

The Economist followed up shortly thereafter in November 2015, publishing a headline: "Black gold under the Golan" with the subtitle: "Geologists in Israel think they have found oil—in very tricky territory."[95] The article stated:

> Israeli and American oilmen believe they have discovered a bonanza in this most inconvenient of sites. After three test-drillings, Yuval Bartov, the chief geologist of Genie Oil & Gas, a subsidiary of American-based Genie Energy, says his company thinks it has found an oil reservoir "with the potential of billions of barrels."

In December 2017, the Jerusalem Post reported that Israel was "Entering a New Era of Natural Gas:"[96]

> Israel is poised to enter a new era of exporting natural gas to her neighbors as well as displacing coal for domestic energy production leading to a healthier future for Israel's citizens, according to Binyamin A. Zomer, Noble Energy's vice president for regional affairs, which operates the Tamar and Leviathan natural-gas fields offshore Israel.
>
> "Israel's ability to export natural gas has provided a common interest for Israel and its neighbors, including Jordan, Egypt, and Turkey," said Zomer. "Natural gas puts Israel in a new position as energy suppliers and not just energy consumers."

---

[95] 2015 November 7, retrieved from https://www.economist.com/news/middle-east-and-africa/21677597-geologists-israel-think-they-have-found-oilin-very-tricky-territory-black-gold

[96] Maayan Hoffman, "Entering a New Era of Natural Gas," 2017 December 10, retrieved from https://www.jpost.com/Israel-News/Entering-a-new-era-of-natural-gas-517621

In February 2018, the *Jerusalem Post* reported: "$15 billion worth of Israeli natural gas to be sold to Egypt."[97] The article noted:

> Prime Minister Benjamin Netanyahu touted the agreements with Egypt as a sign of Israel's burgeoning geopolitical sway, adding that it would benefit state coffers with tax revenue.
>
> "Many did not believe in the gas outline," he said. "We led it forward with the knowledge that it would strengthen our security, strengthen our economy, strengthen regional relations, and above all, it would strengthen the citizens of Israel.... This is a joyous day."

At the same time, *World Oil Magazine* reported a different company's find: "Zion Oil & Gas encounters oil onshore Israel."[98] The article stated:

> Zion Oil & Gas, Inc. announces that during the current open hole wireline logging and subsequent reaming (cleaning the well bore) operations, Zion encountered free-flowing hydrocarbons while circulating drilling mud.
>
> Zion's chief executive officer was quoted as saying: "I am ecstatic to see clear evidence of hydrocarbons (oil and gas) in the deeper portion of our Megiddo-Jezreel #1 well."

Back in October 2015, even the *Russian Times* reported on the magnitude of Afek Oil and Gas's discovery,[99] noting that:

---

[97]   Max Schindler, "$15 Billion Worth of Israeli Natural Gas to Be Sold to Egypt," 2018 February 19, retrieved from https://www.jpost.com/Israel-News/Israeli-gas-company-will-export-gas-worth-15-billion-to-Egypt-543025

[98]   http://www.worldoil.com/news/2018/2/14/zion-oil-gas-encounters-oil-onshore-israel

[99]   "Huge oil discovery in Golan Heights—Israeli media," 2015 October 7, retrieved from https://www.rt.com/business/317906-oil-golan-heights-israel/

The reported discovery coincides with the civil war raging in Syria. Israel has been accused of taking advantage of the conflict. The Israeli-occupied Golan Heights also border Syrian territory controlled by antigovernment rebels. Israel has reportedly provided medical aid to the rebels and has responded to rocket fire from rebel-controlled territory by striking Syrian Army positions. Israel's explanation has been that it "holds the Syrian military responsible for all events stemming from its territory."

Awareness of this discovery might partly explain why Russia has so adamantly propped up the Assad regime in Syria. The scenario predicted in Ezekiel 36-39 appears to be taking shape as Russia moves more military assets into and close to Syria. As Ezekiel predicted some 2,600 years ago, Gog (Russia) will invade Israel with the prime motivation of seizing spoil and carrying off plunder (Ezekiel 38:12). Oil—which remains a necessity for most of the world—is worthy of being plundered.

God's Judgment on Gog-Magog Invasion

What might take place after this? The Bible has revealed the outcome of this allied invasion of Israel:

- "I [the Lord God] will execute judgment on him [Gog the leader of Magog, ie. Russia] with plague and bloodshed; I will pour down torrents of rain, hailstones and burning sulfur on him and on his troops and on the many nations with him" (Ezekiel 38:22, NIV).
- In the aftermath, Israelis will bury the bodies of the fallen armies of Magog [Russia] and its allies. The task will be so enormous that it will take over seven months to complete (Ezekiel 39:11-14).
- "And so I will show my greatness and my holiness, and I will

make myself known in the sight of many nations. Then they will know that I am the Lord" (Ezekiel 38:23, NIV).

As an aside, Russia's gross domestic product (GDP) was only 1,283.20 billion US dollars in 2016. That was a tiny fraction of the US GDP at 18,624.48 billion US dollars in 2016. Russia's GDP represented 2.07 percent of the world economy. Russia's per capita annual income in 2016 was 11,099.20 US dollars, as compared with the US per capita income of 52,194.90 **US dollars**.[100] Trump's bombshell withdrawal from the Iran nuclear agreement will likely affect worldwide oil prices, thereby benefiting the Russian economy. However, the impact is unlikely to single-handedly give Russia the economic power to support its desired role as a political superpower.

Russia has played a much larger role than it can sustain. The Russian invasion of the Holy Land will be doomed, especially with God's promised divine protection of His Chosen People.

So whatever audacious geopolitical manoeuvres Russia attempts under Putin or his successors, the outcomes were prophesied more than 2,600 years ago. How awesome to see that the Bible foresaw the rise of Russia and the coalition involving Iran that Russia will lead in attacking the Holy Land. These hastening footsteps should tell us that He is coming back soon. Amen. Come, Lord Jesus.

How soon is "Soon"?

CHAPTER 4

THE ISRAELIS AND THIRD TEMPLE BOMBSHELLS

In May 2018, the US embassy in Jerusalem was officially opened—after moving from Tel-Aviv which is undisputedly within Israel. The British newspaper *The Guardian*, reported that a celebratory atmosphere greeted the move to Jerusalem,[101] echoing the words of Israeli newspaper *Haaretz*: "In Israel these days, Benjamin Netanyahu is king and Donald Trump is a god." The latter comment refers to Israeli Prime Minister Netanyahu's March 2018 remarks comparing US President Trump to an ancient Persian ruler credited with helping the Jews to return from exile.[102] (Comparisons between Trump and the Persian ruler Cyrus are further discussed below). The US embassy's move can be seen

---

[101] Oliver Holmes, 2018 May 11, "Israel at 70: jubilant US embassy opening masks fevered times," https://www.theguardian.com/world/2018/may/11/us-embassy-opening-israel-at-70

[102] Andrew Silow-Carroll, 2018 March 8, Who is King Cyrus, and why did Netanyahu compare him to Trump? https://www.timesofisrael.com/who-is-king-cyrus-and-why-is-netanyahu-comparing-him-to-trump/
       See also Isaiah chapters 44 and 45; Ezra 1 and 6; 2 Chronicles 36

as one of two gifts from Trump to Israel, the other being his withdrawal from the Iran nuclear deal just five days earlier.[103]

Leading up to the embassy's move, a University of Maryland poll of Jewish Israelis found that 73 percent of them supported the embassy move, including its timing.[104] Two Christian pastors spoke at the new embassy's inauguration ceremony. Robert Jeffress prayed: "Israel has blessed this world by pointing us to you, the one true God, through the message of her prophets, the Scriptures, and the Messiah."[105] And John Hagee delivered the closing benediction: "The Messiah will come and establish a kingdom that will never end."

Mark Twain's Pauper Holy Land

For centuries, the idea of the Jewish people returning to the land of their forefathers seemed absurd to most of the world. In 1869, classic American author Mark Twain shared his humourous take on the Holy Land, which he had visited two years earlier:[106]

- Chapter 47: "We traversed some miles of desolate country whose soil is rich enough, but is given over wholly to weeds—a silent, mournful expanse...."
- Chapter 49: "A desolation is here that not even imagination

[103] Oliver Holmes, 2018 May 11, "Israel at 70: jubilant US embassy opening masks fevered times," https://www.theguardian.com/world/2018/may/11/us-embassy-opening-israel-at-70

[104] Shibley Telhami, "Poll: Jewish Israelis love Trump," 2018 May 15, https://www.brookings.edu/blog/order-from-chaos/2018/05/15/poll-jewish-israelis-love-trump/

[105] Jamie Seidel, 2018 May 16, "Middle Eastern prophecy: Is Trump King Cyrus reincarnated, destined to herald the end of days?," https://www.nzherald.co.nz/world/news/article.cfm?c_id=2&objectid=12052786

[106] Mark Twain, 1869, *Innocents Abroad* (original chapter numbering; subsequently the book was divided into two parts, and the latter chapters were renumbered).

can grace with the pomp of life and action.... We never saw a human being on the whole route."

- Chapter 56: "Renowned Jerusalem itself, the stateliest name in history, has lost all its ancient grandeur, and is become a pauper village; the riches of Solomon are no longer there to compel the admiration of visiting Oriental queens; the wonderful temple which was the pride and the glory of Israel is gone...."

Newton Believed the Jews Would Return to the Promised Land

Yet the great scientist Isaac Newton, as part of his intensive studies on Bible prophecies, interpreted the prophecies to mean that the Jews would return to the Holy Land before the world ends. The end of days will see "the ruin of the wicked nations, the end of weeping and of all troubles, the return of the Jews captivity and their setting up a flourishing and everlasting Kingdom."[107]

Stephen Snobelen has written extensively about Isaac Newton's science and his theology.[108] In a 2001 book chapter, Snobelen wrote:

Newton believed that prophecies relating to the return of the Jews abound in Scripture—particularly in the Hebrew Prophets. Accordingly, in several places in his manuscripts, he writes out long lists of biblical references to prophecies concerning the return of the Jews. He asserts ... confidently in a later writing that such predictions occurred in "all the old Prophets."

---

[107] Matti Friedman, 2007 June 19, "Papers Reveal Isaac Newton's Religious Side," https://www.livescience.com/1638-papers-reveal-isaac-newton-religious-side.html

[108] See for example his faculty profile at the University of King's College, Halifax, Canada: https://ukings.ca/people/stephen-d-snobelen/

CHRIST'S RETURN AND TODAY'S GLOBAL GEOPOLITICAL BOMBSHELLS

Newton believed that the Jews are God's chosen people, unique among the nations and special recipients of divine grace, referring to them as "{God's} people the Jews."

Newton based his conviction in the Jews' unique status particularly on the Abrahamic Covenant, which affirms the special blessed position of Abraham and his seed (Genesis 12:1-3), as well as the promise to them of the land of Canaan (Genesis 13:14-17). After telling him to survey the land, God tells Abraham: "For all the land which thou seest, to thee will I give it, and to thy seed for ever" (Genesis 13:15).[109]

God promised in Amos 9:14-15:

14 And I will bring again the captivity of my people of Israel, and they shall build the waste cities, and inhabit them; and they shall plant vineyards, and drink the wine thereof; they shall also make gardens, and eat the fruit of them. 15 And I will plant them upon their land, and they shall no more be pulled up out of their land which I have given them, saith the LORD thy God. (KJV)

Reclaiming the Land of Their Forefathers

Amazingly, in 1948 after being exiled by the Romans nineteen centuries earlier,[110] the people of Israel were finally able to reclaim the land of their forefathers.

---

[109] S. Snobelen, 2001, "'The Mystery of This Restitution of All Things': Isaac Newton on the Return of the Jews." pp.98–99, in J.E. Force and R.H. Popkin (eds.), *Millenarianism and Messianism in Early Modern European Culture: The Millenarian Turn*, available from https://isaacnewtonstheology.files.wordpress.com/2013/06/isaac-newton-on-the-return-of-the-jews.pdf

[110] See for example "Second Jewish Revolt," https://www.britannica.com/event/Second-Jewish-Revolt
and "Origins of a modern Jewish state," https://www.britannica.com/place/Israel/History#ref219417

Cecil Roth is known to many for his book, *The History of the Jews*.[111] The Jewish education organization Aish HaTorah[112] mentions the book in an article about the miracles of Israel.[113] The article describes Roth as "an Oxford professor and nonobservant Jew," who nonetheless wrote the following at the end of his book:

> In a reading of Jewish history, one factor emerges which may perhaps help us in our decision: the preservation of the Jew was certainly not casual. He has endured through the power of a certain ideal, based upon the recognition of the influence of a ~~higher power in human~~ El Shaddai affairs. Indeed, time after time in his history he has been saved from disaster in a manner which cannot be described as anything but ~~providential.~~ Divine

This author has deliberately attempted to write this book in a secular spirit, but he does not think that his readers can fail to see on every page a higher immanence.

Prompted by Roth's concession, the Aish authors remark:

> Obviously, when Cecil Roth looked at history, just as you're looking at it now, he saw the impossible contradictions: an eternal nation, exiled and dispersed throughout the globe; subject to intense anti-Semitism which should assure their extinction; few in number, and yet, despite that, a light unto the nations. One contradiction after another. The land produces nothing when their enemies inhabit it, yet when the Jews return, the desert blooms once again.

---

[111] 1954, reprinted multiple times

[112] "About Us," http://www.aish.com/about/?s=nb

[113] Rabbi Motty Berger and Rabbi Asher Resnick, "Seven Wonders of Jewish History," www.aish.com/jl/h/h/48965856.html

Israel, a Nation of Miracles

Beyond their return to the homeland seventy years ago, Israel has continued to be a nation of miracles—including miracles that the Bible foretold. One area of miraculous prophecy-fulfilment is Israel's military strength despite being a small nation.

Several times in the Bible, the Lord promises to defend Israel during armed conflict and put Israel's enemies to shame. For example:

- Zechariah 12:8–9: "8 "In that day the LORD will defend the inhabitants of Jerusalem, and the one who is feeble among them in that day will be like David, and the house of David will be like God, like the angel of the LORD before them. 9 And in that day I will set about to destroy all the nations that come against Jerusalem." (NASB)
- Ezekiel 37:9–10: "9 Then He said to me, "Prophesy to the breath, prophesy, son of man, and say to the breath, 'Thus says the Lord GOD, "Come from the four winds, O breath, and breathe on these slain, that they come to life."'" 10 So I prophesied as He commanded me, and the breath came into them, and they came to life and stood on their feet, an exceedingly great army." (NASB)
- Isaiah 41:12-14: "12 Those who war with you will be as nothing and non-existent. 13 For I am the LORD your God, who upholds your right hand, Who says to you, 'Do not fear, I will help you.' 14 Do not fear, you worm Jacob, you men of Israel; I will help you," declares the LORD, "and your Redeemer is the Holy One of Israel." (NASB)

In the lead-up to Israel's declaration of statehood, the United Nations (UN) General Assembly deliberated over a plan to partition Palestine into Jewish and Arab portions. While most Zionists accepted the plan, practically all Arab nations rejected it. Palestinian representative Jamal

still going on

Husseini "announced that if the UN tried to implement partition, 'the blood will flow like rivers in the Middle East.'"[114]

Facing a War of Extermination and a Massacre

The UN adopted the partition plan, but before it could be implemented, civil war broke out between Jews and Arabs within Palestine. The conflict continued through Israel's declaration of independence (May 14, 1948), becoming the Arab-Israeli War. The war pitted a handful of Arab League nations against the nascent Israel. Iraq's then-prime minister promised: "We will smash the country with our guns, and destroy and obliterate every place the Jews will seek shelter in."[115] Syria's then-president stated: "We shall eradicate Zionism."[116] Abdul Rahman Azzam, then-secretary general to the Arab League, declared: "I personally wish that the Jews do not drive us to this war, as this will be a war of extermination and a momentous massacre which will be spoken of like the Mongolian massacres and the Crusades."[117]

Outsiders estimated that Israel could not withstand the Arab League's assault. According to Benny Morris's book *1948: A History of the First Arab-Israeli War*:

---

[114] See for example Sol Stern, 2011, *A Century of Palestinian Rejectionism and Jew Hatred* (Encounter Books) at p.1942

[115] See for example Gabriel G. Tabarani, 2008, *Israeli-Palestinian Conflict: from Balfour Promise to Bush Declaration: The Complications and the Road for a Lasting Peace* (AuthorHouse) p.77
    and Mizra Khan, 2016, "The Arab Refugees—A Study in Frustration," in Walter Z. Laqueur, ed., *The Middle East in Transition: Studies in Contemporary History* (Taylor & Francis), p.240

[116] See for example Benny Morris, 2008, *1948: a history of the first Arab-Israeli war* (Yale University Press) p.187

[117] See for example David Barnett and Efraim Karsh, 2011, "Azzam's Genocidal Threat" in *Middle East Quarterly* Fall 2011, retrieved from https://www.meforum.org/articles/2011/azzam-s-genocidal-threat
    and Mizra Khan, 2016, "The Arab Refugees—A Study in Frustration," in Walter Z. Laqueur, ed., *The Middle East in Transition: Studies in Contemporary History* (Taylor & Francis), p.237

At the start of the civil war, Whitehall [Britain's public service including the Ministry of Defence] believed that the Arabs would prevail. "In the long run the Jews would not be able to cope ... and would be thrown out of Palestine unless they came to terms with [the Arabs]," was the considered judgment of the chief of the Imperial General Staff (CIGS) [head of the British Army].[118]

The consensus in the US government departments was that the Arab states would attack the Jewish state and persist in a guerilla war for as long as it took.... Without "diplomatic and military support" from at least one Great Power, the Jewish state would go under within "two years," they believed.[119]

The Miracle of the War of Independence

Regarding the Arab fighting force, Martin Van Creveld's book, *The Sword and the Olive: A Critical History of the Israeli Defense Force*, states:[120]

> In the [actual] event the invading [Arab] forces were limited to approximately 30,000 men.... Thus, even though the Arab countries outnumbered the Yishuv [the Jewish population] by better than forty-to-one, in terms of military manpower available for combat in Palestine the two sides were fairly evenly matched. As time went on and both sides sent in reinforcements the balance changed in the Jews' favor; by October 1948 they had almost 90,000 men and women under arms, the Arabs only 68,000.

---

[118] Benny Morris, 2008, *1948: a history of the first Arab-Israeli war* (Yale University Press) p.81

[119] Benny Morris, 2008, *1948: a history of the first Arab-Israeli war* (Yale University Press) p.174

[120] Martin Van Creveld, 1998, *The Sword and the Olive: A Critical History of the Israeli Defense Force* (PublicAffairs) pp.77-78

Both sides were short on weapons, but the Jews were better-organized, more unified, and likely more motivated.

In early 1949, Israel entered armistice agreements with its neighbouring Arab states—agreements which granted Israel more territory than the UN's partition plan.[121] Israelis know the war as the War of Independence, but Arabs know the humiliating defeat as al-Nakba (the Catastrophe).[122]

Given the prewar outlook which heavily favoured the Arab nations, it seems that the differences between the Israeli and Arab capabilities were not known until afterward—except the Lord, the God of Israel knew it all. As noted above, the Lord had promised long ago to defend Israel and defeat its enemies through Zechariah, Ezekiel, and others.

Israel has also prevailed in other military contests throughout the years, including the Six-Day War of June 5–10, 1967. The 1948 Arab-Israeli War had left the old city of Jerusalem divided between Jewish and Arab (Jordanian) control. In the following decades, Jewish people could not pray at the Western Wall overlooked by the Temple Mount—site of the ancient temples. Tensions continued between Israel and its Arab neighbours.

The Miracle of the Six-Day War

There is a link to Chapter 2 of the present book regarding the Yankee Going Home scenario. The US was not Israel's single greatest ally in 1967, but the Soviet Union perceived that the US-Israel relationship was warm. The Soviets wanted to make more trouble for the US, which was already entangled in Vietnam. So in May 1967, the Soviets warned

---

[121] See infographic (map) by Good and Column Five, 2011, "Palestine's Shifting Borders: Cartographic Regression," https://www.good.is/infographics/infographic-palestine-s-shifting-borders

[122] The term 'al-Nakba' was coined by Syrian Arab Constantine Zurayq, who is reputedly a Christian. See for example "Why the Arabs were defeated," 2009 July 13, https://www.aljazeera.com/focus/arabunity/2008/02/200852518398869597.html

Egypt that Israel was massing troops on the border with Syria and would attack shortly.[123] Egypt, Jordan, Syria, and Iraq prepared to go to war.

Iraq's then-president declared: "The existence of Israel is an error which must be rectified. This is our opportunity to wipe out the ignominy which has been with us since 1948. Our goal is clear—to wipe Israel off the map."[124]

But according to Jeremy Bowen writing for the BBC (British Broadcasting Corporation), the US did not want to intervene militarily; when consulted by Israel's foreign minister, US President Lyndon Johnson "warned Israel not to fire the first shot,[125]". Although Israeli leadership was reluctant to go against the combined Arab forces, privately Israel's military generals were confident that if they acted quickly they could succeed.

Before the Arab nations could act, Israel moved preemptively the morning of June 5, 1967. Bowen writes:

> The Israeli war plan depended on a surprise attack, called Operation Focus, which would destroy the Arab air forces on the ground, starting with Egypt.
>
> Unlike the Egyptians and the other Arab armies, the Israelis had done their homework. They had flown hundreds of reconnaissance missions over the years to build up an accurate picture of every airbase in Egypt, Jordan, and Syria....
>
> Later in the day Israel destroyed most of the Jordanian and Syrian air forces. Israel controlled the skies, and after that it was matter of finishing the job.

---

[123] See for example Jeremy Bowen, 2017 June 5, "1967 war: Six days that changed the Middle East," www.bbc.com/news/world-middle-east-39960461

[124] See for example Mark A. Tessler, *A History of the Israeli-Palestinian Conflict*

[125] See for example Jeremy Bowen, 2017 June 5, "1967 war: Six days that changed the Middle East," www.bbc.com/news/world-middle-east-39960461

Commemorating the 50th anniversary of the Six-Day War, in May 2017 a Messianic Jewish[126] magazine summarized "God's miraculous intervention" during the war:[127]

> As the Israeli Air Force took to the sky, the first miracle of the war occurred. Jordanian radar detected the planes and tried to warn Egypt, but the Egyptians had changed their coding frequencies the previous day and had not yet updated the Jordanians with the new codes. The message never went through, giving Israel the element of surprise. The Israeli Air Force destroyed six Egyptian airfields and hundreds of Egyptians planes. In a single day, Israel destroyed the Egyptian and Syrian Air Forces. The Egyptian Air Force never even had a chance to leave the ground.
>
> That same day, the Israelis launched a ground offensive into the Gaza Strip and the Sinai, catching Egyptian troops completely by surprise.... The speed of the Israeli advance placed at least one Israeli tank crew in a vulnerable position. They found themselves lost in the Sinai and surrounded by Egyptian posts. The tank commander prayed, "HaShem [or Yahweh],[128] you led our ancestors through this wilderness with a pillar of fire. Please show us the path on which you led our fathers out from this place." Incredibly, the crew spotted a ridgeway, as if illuminated from above, that led them through the rugged territory, away from enemy posts, and back to safety.
>
> On the first day of the war, the Israeli ground forces had overrun the strategic road junction at Abu-Ageila to gain access

---

[126] Messianic Judaism seeks to reconcile Judaism's Torah with biblical scriptures about the Messiah.

[127] D. Thomas Lancaster, 2017 May 14," Miracles of the Six-Day War" in *Messiah Magazine*, First Fruits of Zion, 800.775.4807, www.ffoz.org, https://ffoz.org/discover/messiah-magazine/miracles-of-the-six-day-war.html

[128] HaShem is a common way for Jewish people to refer to God instead of the name YHWH (Yahweh). See for example Jon Dabach, "Hashem: The Name," www.aish.com/sp/ph/69739762.html

to the central route into the Sinai Desert, sending a wave of panic through the Egyptian command. In Bible times, God often assisted the people of Israel on the battlefield by throwing the Canaanites, Philistines, Arameans, and other enemies into panic and confusion. The Torah says, "I will send my terror before you and will throw into confusion all the people against whom you shall come" (Exodus 23:27-28)....

Several Bible stories tell about Israel's enemies succumbing to a supernaturally induced panic and fleeing so quickly that they left their equipment and supplies strewn behind them... (2 Kings 7:15). A similar supernatural terror befell the Egyptian army ... the Egyptian minister of defense ... inexplicably ordered all his units in the Sinai to retreat.... Israeli ground troops advancing into the Sinai found numerous Egyptian positions simply abandoned, with tanks and heavy armor left in perfect condition. They acquired so much abandoned Egyptian armor that after the war they had enough to outfit five new brigades.

The stark outcome for Egypt is consistent with the prophecy in Ezekiel 29:14–15:

14 I will turn the fortunes of Egypt and ... they will be a lowly kingdom. 15 It will be the lowest of the kingdoms, and it will never again lift itself up above the nations. And I will make them so small that they will not rule over the nations. (NASB)

In the next few days, Israel went on to attack Syria. By the end of the war, Israel controlled the remainder of historic Palestine (thus Jerusalem was unified) as well as the Egyptian Sinai desert (Sinai Peninsula) and the Golan Heights from Syria.[129]

---

[129] See for example "The October Arab-Israeli War of 1973: What happened?," 2017 October 8, https://www.aljazeera.com/indepth/features/2017/10/arab-israeli-war-of-1973-what-happened-171005105247349.html

The Miracle of Survival through the Yom Kippur War

Stung by defeats in 1948 and 1967, Israel's Arab neighbours launched an offensive in October 1973. In what is "known to Israelis as the Yom Kippur War, and to Arabs as the October War,"[130] each side experienced some victories.

Reversing the script from the Six-Day War, this time Egypt and Syria coordinated two fronts of surprise attacks on Israel. They chose to attack on Yom Kippur, Judaism's holiest day, when Jewish society is effectively shut down for fasting and repentance.[131] By this time, the Soviet Union had been supplying Arab nations with weapons and the US was solidly in Israel's camp.

On the afternoon of October 6, 1973, Egyptian forces moving eastward reclaimed the Sinai Peninsula while Syrian forces moving southwest reclaimed the Golan Heights. By the next day, Moshe Dayan, Israel's minister of Defense and a hero of the 1967 Six-Day War, was "transformed into a prophet of doom" who feared the imminent demise of the "Third Temple," which in the circumstances likely referred to the modern state of Israel.[132]

In October 2010, the Israeli government declassified and granted public access to the minutes of confidential meetings among Israeli leadership at the start of the 1973 war. An article in the *New York Times* stated:[133]

---

[130] See for example "The October Arab-Israeli War of 1973: What happened?," 2017 October 8, https://www.aljazeera.com/indepth/features/2017/10/arab-israeli-war-of-1973-what-happened-171005105247349.html

[131] See for example Kevin Connolly, 2013 October 5, Legacy of 1973 Arab-Israeli war reverberates 40 years on, www.bbc.com/news/world-middle-east-24402464

[132] See for example Avner Cohen, 2013 October 3, "When Israel Stepped Back From the Brink," https://www.nytimes.com/2013/10/04/opinion/when-israel-stepped-back-from-the-brink.html

[133] See for example Ethan Bronner, 2010 October 10, "Transcripts on '73 War, Now Public, Grip Israel," https://www.nytimes.com/2010/10/11/world/middleeast/11israel.html

The transcripts of the meetings show Mr. Dayan, the unflappable ... defense minister, at the edge of desperation. As Syrian tanks rolled toward the Galilee unimpeded, he understood that he had misread the signals.

"I underestimated the enemy's strength, I overestimated our own forces," he is quoted as saying in an early meeting with Prime Minister Golda Meir and others. "The Arabs are much better soldiers than they used to be."

Then: "Many people will be killed."

An Orthodox Jewish magazine offered more detail:[134]

Perusing those minutes, one realizes just how much trouble the country was in at that time. The crisis could have led to the destruction of Israel as a state.

The minutes of those meetings on those first days of tragic casualties, while Egypt advanced steadily into Sinai.... Golda Meir was actually contemplating suicide, and legendary Defense Minister Moshe Dayan admitted ... that he did not know what to do at that critical hour.

Reading all these facts, one is deeply shaken ... the whole population of Israel at that time was in a storm-tossed ship without a captain!

But what of the Bible's prophecies that Israel would stand strong against its enemies?

An article by the Al Jazeera Media Network[135] describes the subsequent events of 1973:

---

[134] Amir Oren, "Newly Released Documents Shed Light on Fateful Exchange in the Wake of the Yom Kippur War," https://www.haaretz.com/1.5216781

[135] See for example "The October Arab-Israeli War of 1973: What happened?," 2017

The Israeli losses were heavy and the course of the war seemed to [lie] squarely within Arab hands.

But in less than 24 hours, Israel had mobilised two armoured divisions, which soon turned the Syrian advance into a retreat.

As a result, units from the Iraqi, Saudi, and Jordanian armies joined the fight on the Syrian front to face the counterattack. Still, the Israelis manage to achieve significant gains—advancing to within 35 km of Damascus.

On October 16, ten days after the start of the war, Israeli forces … came within a shocking distance from Cairo, the Egyptian capital city.

Israel's success over several Arab foes is consistent with the Lord's promises to protect Israel against its enemies. Israel was aided when the US—which was initially reluctant to intervene—saw the Soviets supporting the Arabs and decided to supply Israel with superior weapons.[136]

One particular miracle of this war took place on the fourth day of tank battles in the Golan Heights. For three days, the Israelis had managed to hold off vastly more numerous Syrian tanks and artillery. In his aforementioned book *The Sword and the Olive*, Martin Van Creveld describes a sudden turn of events:[137]

> On the morning of October 9 the situation of [Israel's] 7th Armored Brigade became desperate when the Syrians … was equipped with T-62 tanks, the most powerful in the Arab arsenal … matching the Israeli 105 mm guns.
>
> In particular, the tanks of one battalion—Col. Avigdor

October 8, https://www.aljazeera.com/indepth/features/2017/10/arab-israeli-war-of-1973-what-happened-171005105247349.html

[136] See for example Jeremy Bowen, 2017 June 5, "1967 war: Six days that changed the Middle East," www.bbc.com/news/world-middle-east-39960461

[137] Martin Van Creveld, 1998, *The Sword and the Olive: A Critical History of the Israeli Defense Force* (PublicAffairs) pp.231-232

Kahalani's 77th—were down to their last few rounds of ammunition. Then suddenly the Syrian rear echelons turned around and retreated, followed by the tanks in the forward line.

The Syrian retreat, which, judging from the way it proceeded, must have been ordered from above, have never been made clear.

From a biblical perspective, the Syrian retreat was certainly "ordered from above"—ordered by the Lord, in fulfilment of His promises from long ago!

By October 16, the fighting had reached a stalemate. The Arab nations pledged to reduce their oil production for as long as Israeli forces occupied the lands won in the 1967 war. To punish the US for supporting Israel, the Arab nations also suspended oil supplies to the US. By the final week of October 1973, each side of the war was ready to negotiate a ceasefire. The US engaged actively in diplomatic efforts. Eventually, a series of agreements was signed and the oil embargo was lifted.[138]

Moving beyond the miraculously-fulfilled prophecies over the nation of Israel, the question arises: Why is Israel (particularly Jerusalem) important for biblical end-time prophecy?

Jerusalem and the Third Temple

Jerusalem is not only the 'City of Peace'[139] and the holy city of Jews, Christians, and Muslims. It is also the home of Abraham and David; and it is where Jesus died, where he was resurrected, and where he will return in glory.

---

[138] See for example "The October Arab-Israeli War of 1973: What happened?," 2017 October 8, https://www.aljazeera.com/indepth/features/2017/10/arab-israeli-war-of-1973-what-happened-171005105247349.html

[139] It is said that the word Jerusalem (in Hebrew Yerushalem or Yerushalayim) is a combination of Ir ('the city') or Yireh ('the abiding place'), and Shalem ('place of peace').

What about the Third Temple? As noted above, in some contexts the phrase "Third Temple" might refer to the modern state of Israel. In other cases, it refers to a future rebuilt temple that some Israelis wish to arrange. As far back as the sixth century BC when the Babylonians conquered Jerusalem and destroyed the first temple, Jewish people have been praying for a rebuilt temple. During Daniel's exile to Babylon, for example, he set a precedent by praying: "Cause thy face to shine upon thy sanctuary that is desolate, for the Lord's sake" (Daniel 9:17b, KJV). In the same vein, the psalmist cried out: "If I forget thee, O Jerusalem, let my right hand forget her cunning. If I do not remember thee, let my tongue cleave to the roof of my mouth; if I prefer not Jerusalem above my chief joy" (Psalm 137:5-6, KJV). And since AD 70 when the Romans destroyed the second temple, Orthodox Jews have recited three times daily a prayer to the effect of 'May it be your will, Oh God, that the Temple be speedily rebuilt in our day, and there we shall reverently worship You, as we did in days of old.'

Various passages in the Old and New Testaments have been interpreted to mean that a new temple will exist as part of God's end-time prophecy. See for example Ezekiel 37:26–28 and 40–48; Daniel 9:24–27; Micah 4:1–2; Zechariah 6:12–15 and 14:20; Matthew 24:15; Mark 13:14; 2 Thessalonians 2:4; and Revelation 11:1–2. Fully reclaiming the ancient temple site for Israel would be an important step toward building a Third Temple.

US Embassy Relocation Bombshell and Comparisons with Cyrus

This is partly why in December 2017, when US President Trump issued his order to move the US Embassy to Jerusalem, Israeli Prime Minister Benjamin Netanyahu reportedly said:

This is a historic day.... We're profoundly grateful for the president for his courageous and just decision to recognize Jerusalem as the capital of Israel and to prepare for the opening of the US embassy here."[140]

Netanyahu was also reported as saying, "The Jewish people and the Jewish state will be forever grateful" for Trump's decision amid outcry from Arab leaders.[141]

In March 2018 while visiting President Trump in Washington, DC, Prime Minister Netanyahu was reported as comparing Trump with the historical figure, King Cyrus:[142]

> The Jewish people have a long memory, so we remember the proclamation of the great king, Cyrus the Great, the Persian king 2,500 years ago. He proclaimed that the Jewish exiles in Babylon could come back and rebuild our Temple in Jerusalem.... And we remember how a few weeks ago, President Donald J. Trump recognized Jerusalem as Israel's capital.

In Isaiah 45, God chose Cyrus "To subdue nations before him... So that you may know that it is I, The LORD, the God of Israel..." (NASB). The *Times of Israel* also explained:

> The first-century historian Josephus also credits Cyrus with freeing the Jews from captivity and helping them rebuild the temple in Jerusalem.

---

[140] Tamar Pileggi, 2017 December 6, "US, Israel gird for backlash as Trump Jerusalem move roundly condemned," https://www.timesofisrael.com/liveblog-december-6-2017/

[141] Alexandra Wilts, 2017 December 6, "Benjamin Netanyahu thanks Donald Trump for recognising Jerusalem as Israel's capital amid outcry from Arab leaders," https://www.independent.co.uk/news/world/americas/us-politics/jerusalem-is-rael-trump-netanyahu-thanks-us-president-middle-east-latest-a8096066.html

[142] Andrew Silow-Carroll, 2018 March 8, "Who is King Cyrus, and why did Netanyahu compare him to Trump?," https://www.timesofisrael.com/who-is-king-cyrus-and-why-is-netanyahu-comparing-him-to-trump/

In May 2018, the *New Zealand Herald* published a report titled: "Middle Eastern prophecy: Is Trump King Cyrus reincarnated, destined to herald the end of days?"[143] The article explains:

> To Trump's evangelicals, the move to Jerusalem isn't about worldly politics. It's a move that will facilitate prophecy.
>
> The Jews will get to demolish Islam's Dome of the Rock and Al-Aqsa Mosque, and get to build the third incarnation of their sacred temple. (The first was destroyed by the Babylonians, and the second the Romans). This, in turn, will herald Armageddon.
>
> [According to one religious scholar,] "Most evangelicals subscribe to a belief in premillennialism, the belief that the second coming of Christ will begin a 1,000-year period where Christ will rule over a peaceful and prosperous Earth."

In September 2018, the *Jerusalem Post* reported: "Evangelical Christians see Trump as man of God:"[144] "In defending Trump, religious supporters cite a recurring theme in the Bible that God uses flawed leaders." A Baptist missions director was quoted as saying: "King Cyrus was a friend to the people of God, but he was a heathen king." Another pastor was quoted as saying:

> God is using Trump for his own purposes.... The president has taken a stand for life. Second, the president has taken up for Israel and has declared Jerusalem the capital of Israel. Third, he has chosen Supreme Court justices—that's going to turn this nation around.

---

[143] Jamie Seidel, 2018 May 16, "Middle Eastern prophecy: Is Trump King Cyrus reincarnated, destined to herald the end of days?" https://www.nzherald.co.nz/world/news/article.cfm?c_id=2&objectid=12052786

[144] Greg Garrison/ Alabama Media Group, 2018 September 1, "Evangelical Christians See Trump as 'Man of God'," https://www.jpost.com/American-Politics/Evangelical-Christians-see-Trump-as-man-of-God-566249

Israel Related End Time Prophecies Soon Coming True

A rebuilt Jewish temple is but one facet of Israel's importance for the end times. Israel plays a prominent role in many biblical end-time predictions. What follows is a summary of What Might Take Place After This (not necessarily in chronological order):

- The return of Jewish people to the land of Israel (Deuteronomy 30:3; Isaiah 43:6; Ezekiel 34:11–13; 36:24; 37:1–14). This has already transpired.
- The coming Gog-Magog invasion of Israel most likely led by Russia, in coalition with Iran and mostly Israel-hating Muslim nations as discussed in Chapters 4 and 5 Ezekiel chapters 38-39).
- The coming Rapture (1 Thessalonians 4:16–17, John 14:2–3). This can happen at any time, since the precondition that the Jews return to Israel has been fulfilled.
- The revival of a ten-nation Roman Empire, which will be dealt with in Chapter 8.
- The rise of the Antichrist, who will make a seven-year covenant of "peace" with Israel (Isaiah 28:18; Daniel 9:27). This will be treated in Chapter 8.
- The Third Temple will be rebuilt, as discussed earlier in this Chapter (Daniel 9: 24-27; Matthew 24:15; 2 Thessalonians 2:4; Revelation 11:1–2). The Temple Institute in Jerusalem that is dedicated to planning and preparing for the Third Temple's construction as soon as the Jewish people gain access to the location currently under Muslim control. During the first Gulf War called the Desert Storm, this principal author was praying that Saddam Hussein's missiles would land on the Temple Mount, making way for the construction of the Third Temple. Perhaps God could use the Gog-Magog War to allow the Temple Mount to be cleared for the rebuilding project.

- The Antichrist will make then break his covenant with Israel. The worldwide persecution of the Jewish people will result (Zechariah 11:16; Matthew 24:15, 21, and 6;[145] Revelation 12:13). The Great Tribulation will start at the second half of the Tribulation period (see Matthew 24:15 and 21) after the Abomination of Desolation, which marks the midpoint of the Tribulation (Daniel 9:27). This will be discussed in Chapter 8.
- The Battle of Armageddon will take place at the end of the Tribulation period. This is mentioned in Chapter 7 and further discussed in Chapter 8.
- The return of Christ. Israel will finally recognize Jesus as their Messiah (Zechariah 12:10). Israel will be regenerated, restored, and regathered (Jeremiah 33:8; Ezekiel 11:17; Romans 11:26). Jesus will return and defeat all the nations that come to fight in the Battle of Armageddon, and will reign for 1,000 years from His throne in Jerusalem. After this, a final rebellion will take place followed by the new heavens and new earth, and a new heavenly city called the New Jerusalem.

In 2005, Joel C. Rosenberg, who is renowned for writing about Bible prophecy, released the novel *The Ezekiel Option*.[146] The apocalyptic novel weaves realistic storylines onto the end-time prophecies in Ezekiel chapters 38 and 39. Rosenberg invites the reader to ask: if the prophecies in Ezekiel 36 and 37 have come true (including the rebirth of the State of Israel and the Jewish people's return to the Holy Land after centuries in exile), isn't it conceivable that the next prophecies in Ezekiel 38 and 39 could come true in our lifetime?[147]

---

[145] Matthew 24:15 and 21 have been applied to the Roman Empire's attack of Jerusalem in the year AD 70; however, verse 6 cautions that more is to come: "You will be hearing of wars and rumors of wars. See that you are not frightened, for those things must take place, but that is not yet the end." (NASB)

[146] Joel C. Rosenberg, 2005, *The Ezekiel Option* (Tyndale House Publishers)

[147] See for example Joel C. Rosenberg, 2005 December, "Is *The Ezekiel Option*

We have seen God allow Israel to experience utter despair through Babylonian captivity, exile from the Holy Land, and near-annihilation during the Holocaust. Yet we have also seen God allow the people of Israel to return to the land of their forefathers and to come alive as a mighty army.

These things happened precisely as prophesied over 2,000 years ago. The Bible awesomely reveals What Might Take Place After This. Hopefully we can discern the sound of hastening footsteps telling us that He is coming back soon. Amen. Come, Lord Jesus.

Coming True?" http://laymanswatch.com/LaymansWatch_files/Ezekiel38-39/IsThe EzekialOptionComingTrue.htm

CHAPTER 5

THE MIDDLE EAST BOMBSHELL

The Saudi Royal Family and Wahhabism

In *Proteus: Insights from 2020*, the scenario of "Yankee Going Home"[148] foresees a "Saudi Arabian coup"[149] in which "[t]he Saudi royal family was overthrown."[150] That forecast shocked this principal author.

Although the Saudi royal family has been a strong ally of the United States in the Middle East, the family has zealously propagated a strict (arguably radical) form of Sunni Islam called Wahhabism. Wahhabism is named after its founder Abd al-Wahhab, who advocated a puritanical moral code.

Abd al-Wahhab mandated a dual principle of "loyalty and disavowal." True believers of Islam would not only be loyal to the one true god Allah, but would also disavow (by denying and destroying) any other subject of worship. Alastair Crooke, a former British intelligence agent, has written:[151]

---

[148] Discussed in chapter 2 of this book

[149] *Proteus: Insights from 2020*, 2000 Copernicus Institute, Appendix F, page F-xii

[150] *Proteus: Insights from 2020*, 2000 Copernicus Institute, Appendix F, page F-xvi

[151] Alastair Crooke, 2014 November 2, "Middle East Time Bomb: The Real Aim of ISIS Is to Replace the Saud Family as the New Emirs of Arabia," https://www.huffingtonpost.com/alastair-crooke/isis-aim-saudi-arabia_b_5748744.html

The list of potential subjects condemned as idolatrous worship by Abd al-Wahhab was so extensive that almost all Muslims were at risk of falling under his definition of "unbelievers." They [Muslims] therefore faced a choice: either they convert to Al-Wahhab's vision of Islam—or be killed, their wives and daughters violated, and their possessions confiscated as the spoils of jihad. Even to express doubts about this doctrine, Abd al-Wahhab said, should occasion execution. The list of apostates meriting death included the Shiite, Sufis, and other Muslim denominations, whom Abd al-Wahhab did not consider to be Muslim at all.

The first Saudi state founded in 1744 benefited from loyalty between Abd al-Wahhab and the ruling prince.[152] Generations of the ruling family have maintained a commitment to Wahhabism. Since the 1970s, with its wealth-generating oil bonanza, Saudi Arabia has financed the export of Wahhabi schools and mosques to Pakistan, Africa, Indonesia, Europe, and even the US. Yet they have openly contravened radical Wahhabism in supporting and colluding with the US, which is the most dominant leader of the 'infidels' and Christian 'crusaders,' as well as supporting Egypt and Jordan in signing a peace treaty with their archenemy—Israel.

Viewed from the radical Wahhabi perspective that it continues to export, Saudi Arabia's concurrent collusion with infidels puts the kingdom on a path to devastation by the intense inferno of radicalism.

Radicalism is not a new phenomenon in Europe. Radicalism and violent extremism were hallmarks of nationalist, radicalist, Marxist, and fundamentalist groups from World War I all the way through the Cold War.

---

[152] "Saudi Arabia," last updated 2018 May 12, retrieved from https://www.britannica.com/place/Saudi-Arabia

The US's Role in Supporting Radical Islam

When it comes to Islam, one important accelerant to radicalism can be traced back to US and allied actions in relation to the Soviet-Afghan War (1979–1989).[153] A military coup in 1978 had given rise to a left-wing/communist government in Afghanistan, but they had little popular support and soon faced violent opposition from Islamic anticommunist groups known as 'mujahideen.'[154] In December 1979 as the communist Afghan government faced Islamic insurgents and internal conflict, the Soviet Union intervened by invading Afghanistan to crush the insurgencies and prop up the weak government as well as installing a Soviet loyalist as the new president. In parallel to Cold War divides, the US came to support the anticommunist mujahideen partly through Pakistan and the Gulf nations led by Saudi Arabia.

At that time, the US's foreign policies sought to reestablish US economic and military strength while diminishing the Soviet Union's influence across the world. In July 1979—six months before the Soviets marched into Afghanistan—National Security Advisor Zbigniew Brzezinski convinced US President Jimmy Carter to authorize "nonlethal" aid to the Afghan mujahideen.[155] Zbigniew understood the Soviet intervention as part of a larger plan to gain power in the region.[156] He advised

---

[153] The Soviet-Afghan War (1979-1989) covered the majority of the Afghan War (1978-1992, no Soviet intervention). See for example "Afghan War," https://www.britannica.com/event/Afghan-War

   "Soviet invasion of Afghanistan," https://www.britannica.com/event/Soviet-invasion-of-Afghanistan

[154] Mujahideen is the plural form of the Arabic word 'mujahid' which refers to Muslims who proclaim themselves warriors for Islam. See for example "Mujahideen–Islam" https://www.britannica.com/topic/mujahideen-Islam

[155] Greg Grandin, 2015 September 28, "How One Man Laid the Groundwork for Today's Crisis in the Middle East," https://www.thenation.com/article/how-one-man-laid-the-groundwork-for-todays-crisis-in-the-middle-east/

[156] Douglas MacEchin, 2002, *Predicting the Soviet Invasion of Afghanistan: The Intelligence Community's Record*, https://www.cia.gov/library/center-for-the-study-of-intelligence/csi-publications/books-and-monographs/predicting-the-soviet-invasion-of-afghanistan-the-intelligence-communitys-record/predicting-the-soviet-invasion-of-afghanistan-the-intelligence-communitys-record.html

that the US should publicly express "sympathy" toward the Afghan "independence" forces. Walter B. Slocombe, a member of President Carter's Pentagon administration, agreed and wondered whether US support for Islamic insurgents might succeed in "sucking the Soviets into a Vietnamese quagmire."[157]

In April 1979, an inter-agency committee chaired by Brzezinski instructed the CIA (Central Intelligence Agency) to develop a comprehensive plan for a clandestine war in Afghanistan backed by the US, "ranging from indirect financial assistance to the insurgents" to "weapons support."[158] The Soviet Union deployed tens of thousands of troops into Afghanistan, with the necessary tools of war. But by the early-1980s, the mujahideen were able to neutralize Soviet attacks through the use of US-supplied weaponry.[159]

Meanwhile, Saudi Arabia funded a network of madrassas (Islamic religious schools) in the Pakistan-Afghanistan region.[160] Saudi Arabia and the US financed Pakistan's ISI (Inter-Services Intelligence) in training and arming anti-Soviet mujahideen (or 'jihadis') in Afghanistan. And then-director of the CIA William Casey "committed CIA support to a long-standing ISI initiative to recruit radical Muslims from around the world to come to Pakistan and fight with the Afghan Mujahideen."[161]

In all this, the US might have regarded communism as its greatest foe. But unfortunately supporting Islamic insurgent groups had the nefarious side effect of cultivating Islamic radicalism. In 2004, Stefan

---

[157] Douglas Little, *American Orientalism: The United States and the Middle East Since 1945* (London: Tauris, 2003), p.152

[158] Douglas Little, *American Orientalism: The United States and the Middle East Since 1945* (London: Tauris, 2003), p.152

[159] See for example "Soviet invasion of Afghanistan," https://www.britannica.com/event/Soviet-invasion-of-Afghanistan

[160] See for example "Analysis: Madrassas," https://www.pbs.org/wgbh/pages/frontline/shows/saudi/analyses/madrassas.html

[161] Ahmed Rashid, Taliban: Militant Islam, Oil and Fundamentalism in Central Asia" (Yale University Press), excerpt available at iml.jou.ufl.edu/projects/fall01/Easton/webstuff/whoisosama.html

Halper and Jonathan Clarke published a book called *America Alone: The Neo-Conservatives and the Global Order*. The book provides an overview of the rise of modern terrorism and radical Islam:

> The year 1979 was an important one in the development of today's terror phenomenon.... The crucible for the pan-Islamic movement ... was the jihad against the Soviet invasion of Afghanistan in 1979—where, as is well known, US and British intelligence services were working hand-in-glove with the jihadists, all the while being well aware of the latter's extremist tendencies. By the time that the Soviet Union withdrew from Afghanistan in 1989, a whole generation of religiously inspired terrorists had been produced and subsequently dispersed across the globe.[162]

The extreme bedrock of Saudi-supported Wahhabi Islam, aided by the CIA's use of radicalization as a 'weapon of war' to mobilize Afghan mujahideen against communism, spawned the rise of Islamic jihadi groups such as Al Qaeda, Hamas, ISIS (Islamic State), and other terrorist organizations claiming to fight for Islam. Indeed, when ISIS launched its own madarassas, it adopted Saudi-madarassa textbooks until it could publish its own material.[163] The result: generations of radicals bearing ultraconservative Wahhabi mindsets, motivated to carry out attacks on societies and governments that do not comply with their religious-based ideologies.

---

[162] Stefan Halper and Jonathan Clarke, America Alone: The Neo-Conservatives and the Global Order (2004, Cambridge University Press) p.277

[163] Scott Shane, 2016 August 25, "Saudis and Extremism: 'Both the Arsonists and the Firefighters'" https://www.nytimes.com/2016/08/26/world/middleeast/saudi-arabia-islam.html

Once the genie is out of the bottle, who can force it back in?

In view of the nefarious long-term impacts of the CIA's strategy in the style of 'the enemy of my enemy is my friend,' hopefully the intelligence community would seriously review and drastically overhaul any plans based on this simplistic adage.

Many refer to Islam as a religion of peace. Not only does the Arabic word "Islam" share the same root word as the greeting "salaam" (meaning "peace"), but the Quran (the principal Islamic holy text) also sets constraints on jihad (waging war for the faith).[164] The world's problem is not with peaceful religion but rather with terrorists who advocate offensive violence in the name of a radical kind of Islam. The threat of radical Islam has not yet taken over the world, but the geopolitical situation will worsen if the global community hesitates to act and allows more and more countries to crumple under the radicals' influence.

The Lingering Threat of ISIS

In December 2017, prime minister of Iraq Haider al-Abadi announced the final defeat of ISIS,[165] which had gained prominence from 2013 to 2014 and held territory (by force) in Iraq and Syria. Former ISIS strongholds such as Mosul and Ramadi (Iraq) and Raqqa (Syria) have been liberated. Some ISIS fighters remain in Syria, however,[166] and many have

---

[164] See for example Pooyan Fakhrei, 2016 February 1, "You don't need to look much further than the Quran for proof that Islam is a peaceful religion," https://www.independent.co.uk/voices/you-dont-need-to-look-much-further-than-the-quran-for-proof-that-islam-is-a-peaceful-religion-a6847031.html

[165] See for example Margaret Coker and Falih Hassan, 2017 December 9, "Iraq Prime Minister Declares Victory Over ISIS," https://www.nytimes.com/2017/12/09/world/middleeast/iraq-isis-haider-al-abadi.html

[166] Eric Schmitt, 2017 December 24, "The Hunt for ISIS Pivots to Remaining Pockets in Syria," https://www.nytimes.com/2017/12/24/world/middleeast/last-phase-islamic-state-iraq-syria.html

left Iraq and Syria to return to third countries where they remain a threat to local populations.[167] In a February 2018 article,[168] His Excellency Dr. Hanif Hassan Ali Al Qassim from the United Arab Emirates wrote:

> The "real work" to defeat ISIS and its heinous ideology lies in deradicalizing returning militants and addressing the root-causes that initially provided fertile ground to the rise of radicalism.

Likewise, in February 2018 an Indonesian research institute warned of the "disaster waiting to happen" at a particular detention centre holding over one hundred ISIS sympathizers; in addition to overcrowding, the institute pointed out: "There was no effort to offer counseling against violent extremist ideology to new arrivals."[169] A few months later, in May 2018, ISIS-sympathizer inmates seized part of that very detention centre and killed five guards.

The ISIS terrorist attacks in Paris (November 2015), Brussels (March 2016), London Bridge (June 2017), Indonesia (May 2018), and numerous other places clearly demonstrate the reach of ISIS's ideology and threat far beyond geographic war zones.

According to a blog that gathers statistics and articles/ reports related to Muslim issues in non-Muslim societies,[170] in July 2014 the Saudi-based newspaper *Al-Hayat* reported that "an opinion poll of

---

[167] See for example Eric Schmitt, 2018 February 4, "Thousands of ISIS Fighters Flee in Syria, Many to Fight Another Day," https://www.nytimes.com/2018/02/04/world/middleeast/isis-syria-al-qaeda.html

Joe Cochraine, 2018 May 10, Deadly Uprising by ISIS Followers Shakes Indonesia's Prison System, https://www.nytimes.com/2018/05/10/world/asia/indonesia-prison-riot-islamic-state.html

[168] Hanif Hassan Ali Al Qassi, 2018 February 26, "De-radicalization and the defeat of ISIS," https://wsimag.com/economy-and-politics/36475-de-radicalization-and-the-defeat-of-isis

[169] Joe Cochraine, 2018 May 10, "Deadly Uprising by ISIS Followers Shakes Indonesia's Prison System," https://www.nytimes.com/2018/05/10/world/asia/indonesia-prison-riot-islamic-state.html

[170] "About" Muslim statistics, https://muslimstatistics.wordpress.com/about/

Saudis [was] released on social networking sites, claiming that 92 percent of the target group believes that 'IS conforms to the values of Islam and Islamic law.'"[171] The article stated that the Sakinah Campaign (al-Sakinah), which was launched in order to combat online radicalization,[172] intended to follow up by conducting an independent survey.

In May 2015, Al Jazeera's Arabic-language network[173] conducted an online poll asking in Arabic: "Do you support the organizing victories of the Islamic State in Iraq and Syria (ISIS)?" The poll generated over 38,000 responses with 81 percent voting "YES" and only 19 percent of respondents voting "NO" to supporting ISIS.[174] The article noted:

Al Jazeera Arabic's television audience is largely made up of Sunni Muslims living in the Arab world. Its biggest viewership numbers come from Egypt and Saudi Arabia, along with a large amount of satellite television viewers in the United States, according to research estimates. AlJazeera.net is most popular in Saudi Arabia, the United States, Egypt, Morocco, and Bosnia and Herzegovina, according to [an] analytics site.

In February 2017, Al Jazeera published an opinion piece titled: "Time to tackle ISIL's millions of sympathisers?" According to the author, Rami G. Khouri:

---

[171] English translation by Tyler Huffman, "Saudi poll to reveal public's level of sympathy for IS," 2014 July 22, https://muslimstatistics.wordpress.com/2014/08/24/92-of-saudis-believes-that-isis-conforms-to-the-values-of-islam-and-islamic-law-survey/

[172] Christopher Boucek , 2008 August, "The Sakinah Campaign and Internet Counter-Radicalization in Saudi Arabia," https://ctc.usma.edu/the-sakinah-campaign-and-internet-counter-radicalization-in-saudi-arabia/

[173] The poll was not conducted on Al Jazeera's English-language website, according to "81% of Muslims surveyed support Islamic State ideology–Al Jazeera Arabic Poll," 2015 October, https://muslimstatistics.wordpress.com/2015/10/15/poll-81-of-muslims-around-the-world-support-islamic-state-al-jazeera-arabic-poll/

[174] Jordan Schachtel, 2015 May 25, "Shock Poll: 81% of Al Jazeera Arabic Poll Respondents Support Islamic State," www.breitbart.com/national-security/2015/05/25/shock-poll-81-of-al-jazeera-arabic-poll-respondents-support-isis/

We should focus our attention to a much bigger—and an increasingly clear—reality that perhaps up to 30 or 40 million people across the Arab world express sympathy, support, or approval for ISIL and its actions, based on numerous credible surveys of Arab public opinion.

Polling and analyses over the past decade show that a steady average of 4 to 10 percent of Arab survey respondents express some degree of understanding, sympathy, or outright support for ISIL and al-Qaeda's activities or motives.

The actual percentage of supporters in some countries reaches up to 40 percent or more in some years, and fluctuates widely, in response to current events usually.

With such overwhelming grassroot support in the Arab world including Saudi Arabia, the radical ideals of Sunni Islam (including the extremist Wahhabi branch) exceed the defensive capabilities of the US, its NATO allies, and Russia.

Sunni and Shi'a Terrorism

Meanwhile, Islam's internal Sunni-Shi'a divide might have given an advantage to Sunni-based ISIS. Islam is split into mutually noncompromising Sunni and Shiite sects due to a war over the succession of leadership of the faith that followed the Prophet Mohammad's death in the year 632.[175] Despite risks to their economies and political regimes, the Sunni governments of Saudi Arabia, Turkey, and Jordan[176] largely

---

[175] See for example Mariam Karouny, 2014 April 1, "Apocalyptic prophecies drive both sides to Syrian battle for end of time," www.reuters.com/article/us-syria-crisis-prophecy-insight/apocalyptic-prophecies-drive-both-sides-to-syrian-battle-for-end-of-time-idUSBREA3013420140401

[176] See for example Wilson Center, 2018 January, "ISIS Was Defeated in Syria Is That the End for the Islamists?" www.newsweek.com/isis-was-defeated-syria-end-islamists-767165

kept quiet as Sunni-based ISIS waged war in majority-Shi'a Iraq and in Syria which also has substantial Shi'a numbers.[177]

Yet, the danger of radical Islamic violence exists in both Sunni and Shi'a factions. In December 2008, the US research and policy organization Brookings Institution published a paper about Sunni and Shi'a terrorism.[178] The paper noted that whereas Sunni radicals tend to publicize and amplify their actions, Shi'a terrorists "by and large take a much lower-key approach."

The Brookings paper noted other differences between Sunni radicalism and Shi'a extremism:

- "[Sunni radicals] tend to operate in a continuous, mid-to-high intensity manner, seeing war against infidels and apostates as a perennial condition featuring overlapping waves. Outside of an ongoing ... campaign against Israel, terrorist attacks by Shi'a groups have by and large featured discrete terror campaigns tethered to state and organizational objectives." [This principal author adds that Iran's support extends beyond its nation to include Lebanon's Hezbollah group.]

- "Shi'a terrorists, unlike their Sunni counterparts, enjoy direct state support ... more likely to originate from Iranian embassies, consulates, and state-run businesses ... have shown a much greater propensity to kidnap innocents to barter ... targeted assassinations for specific political gain, rather than the high-casualty killings featured in Sunni terrorism."

Radical Sunni and Shi'a violence have different aims and ideological foundations, but danger arises from each side alike. In April 2014

---

[177] See for example 2016 January, "Sunnis and Shia: Islam's ancient schism," www.bbc.com/news/world-middle-east-16047709

[178] Thomas F. Lynch III, 2008 December, "Sunni and Shi 'a Terrorism: Differences that Matter," https://www.brookings.edu/research/sunni-and-shi-a-terrorism-differences-that-matter/

during the Syrian armed conflict, an article by the Reuters news service explained:[179]

> Both sides [Sunni and Shi'a] emphasize the ultimate goal of establishing an Islamic state which will rule the world before total chaos. Although some Sunni and Shi'ite clerics are privately skeptical of the religious justifications for the war, few in the region express such reservations in public for fear of being misinterpreted as doubters of the prophecies.
>
> [On the Sunni side, mujahideen traveled to northern Syria from Russia, the US, the Philippines, China, Germany, Belgium, Sudan, India and Yemen, and other places.]
>
> "If you think all these mujahideen came from across the world to fight Assad, you're mistaken," said a Sunni Muslim jihadi who ... fights in ... Aleppo [Syria]. "They are all here as promised by the Prophet. This is the war he promised—it is the Grand Battle," he told Reuters, using a word which can also be translated as slaughter.
>
> On the other side, many Shi'ites from Lebanon, Iraq, and Iran are drawn to the war because they believe it paves the way for the return of Imam Mahdi—a descendent of the Prophet who vanished 1,000 years ago and who will reemerge at a time of war to establish global Islamic rule before the end of the world.
>
> According to Shi'ite tradition, an early sign of his return came with the 1979 Iranian revolution, which set up an Islamic state to provide fighters for an army led by the Mahdi to wage war in Syria after sweeping through the Middle East.
>
> [An 8th century Shi'ite imam] said another sign of the

---

[179] Mariam Karouny, 2014 April 1, "Apocalyptic prophecies drive both sides to Syrian battle for end of time," retrieved from www.reuters.com/article/us-syria-crisis-prophecy-insight/apocalyptic-prophecies-drive-both-sides-to-syrian-battle-for-end-of-time-idUSBREA3013420140401. Used by permission of Thomson Reuters.

Mahdi's return would be a battle involving warriors fighting under a yellow banner—the color associated with Lebanon's pro-Assad Hezbollah militia ... when the (forces) with yellow flags fight anti-Shi'ites in Damascus and Iranian forces join them, this is a prelude and a sign of the coming of his holiness.

Murtada, a twenty-seven-year-old Lebanese Shi'ite who regularly goes to Syria to battle against the rebels, says he is not fighting for Assad, but for [Imam Mahdi]. "Even if I am martyred now, when he appears I will be reborn to fight among his army, I will be his soldier," he told Reuters in Lebanon. Murtada, who has fought in Damascus and in the decisive battle last year for the border town of Qusair, leaves his wife and two children when he goes to fight in Syria: "Nothing is more precious than the Imam, even my family. It is our duty."

The power of those prophecies for many fighters on the ground means that the ... conflict is more deeply rooted—and far tougher to resolve—than a simple power struggle between President Bashar al-Assad and his rebel foes.

Furthermore, violent ideologies have attracted not only youth or men, but also women and parental units. In the same month as the above-noted Indonesian detention centre incident (May 2018), Indonesia was rocked by two suicide bombs in which parents detonated themselves and their children.[180] A report by the BBC (British Broadcasting Corporation) observed:

While children have been used as suicide bombers before around the world, it is rare that parents take their own children to die along with them. In previous cases, children have been

---

[180] See for example 2018 May 13, "Surabaya church attacks: One family responsible, police say," www.bbc.com/news/world-asia-44100278 and
2018 May 14, "Surabaya attacks: Parents who bring their children to die," www.bbc.com/news/world-asia-44104887

taken from their families, indoctrinated or drugged, then forced to attack.

One should not underestimate how much ISIS-inspired Muslim radicals are willing to sacrifice for their beliefs. Radical Islamic-based ideologies have far-reaching consequences as they spread through Muslim communities.

How does all this relate to God's promises in the Bible?

First, God has continued to protect His Chosen People. It has been said that in the seventeenth century, the "Sun King" Louis XIV of France asked the great mathematician and philosopher Blaise Pascal to give proof of the existence of miracles—to which Pascal responded without hesitation: "Why, the Jews, your Majesty—the Jews."[181] That answer would have been consistent with Pascal's writings; in *Pensées* (Thoughts), he wrote of the "Advantages of the Jewish people":

> This people are not eminent solely by their antiquity, but are also singular by their duration, which has always continued from their origin till now. For whereas the nations of Greece ... Italy ... Lacedaemon ... Athens ... Rome, and others who came long after have long since perished, these ever remain, and in spite of the endeavours of many powerful kings who have a hundred times tried to destroy them ... they have nevertheless been preserved (and this preservation has been foretold); and extending

---

[181] Some attribute the question to Frederick the Great, King of Prussia. French version: Il est dit qu'au 17e siècle, le roi Louis XIV de France a demandé à Blaise Pascal, le mathématicien et philosophe renommé, de lui donner une preuve de l'existence du surnaturel. Pascal lui à répondu : « Mais les Juifs, Votre Majesté, les Juifs. » See John R. Cross (2011) *Par ce nom: La vie se limite-t-elle à ce qu'on voit?* (BonneSemence Canada / GoodSeed International) p.198, 374

from the earliest times to the latest, their history comprehends in its duration that of all our histories.[182]

According to Benjamin Blech, writing for a history website affiliated with George Washington University: "Pascal is but one of many scholars and students of Jewish history who have been awed by a story that seems inexplicable by the ordinary rules of logic."[183]

Today in the early twenty-first century, it appears that the Sunni-Shi'a divide within Islam has provided Israel with a buffer of peace and security; as Sunni and Shi'a followers engage in conflicts with each other, they are unable to coordinate their resources to jointly attack Israel. The Sunni-Shi'a divide is actually drawing Sunni-led nations such as Saudi Arabia to secretly (or at least warily) align with Israel to fight off Shi'a-based forces such as Iran. The Sunnis' hatred of the Shiites is deeper than their hatred of the Jews.

Now that US President Trump has withdrawn from the Iran nuclear agreement,[184] Iran can be expected to ally with Russia to fight against Israel. Trump's bombshell decision has been acclaimed not only by Israelis[185] but also by Saudi Arabia and its Gulf Coast allies, the

---

[182] In French: « Avantages du peuple juif. ...Ce peuple n'est pas seulement considérable par son antiquité, mais il est encore singulier en sa durée, qui a toujours continué depuis son origine jusqu'à maintenant. Car au lieu que les peuples de Grèce et d'Italie, de Lacédémone, d'Athènes, de Rome, et les autres qui sont venus si longtemps après, soient péris il y a si longtemps, ceux-ci subsistent toujours, et malgré les entreprises de tant de puissants rois qui ont cent fois essayé de les faire périr, ... ils ont toujours été conservés néanmoins, et cette conservation a été prédite ; et s'étendant depuis les premiers temps jusques aux derniers, leur histoire enferme dans sa durée celle de toutes nos histoires. »

[183] Rabbi Benjamin Blech, 2007, "The Miracle of Jewish History," https://historynewsnetwork.org/article/38887

[184] Discussed in Chapter 7

[185] As discussed in Chapter 7; see for example Adam Eliyahu Berkowitz, 2018 May 9, "In Convergence of Prophecy and Politics, President Trump Withdraws from Iran Deal," https://www.breakingisraelnews.com/107375/in-convergence-of-prophecy-and-politics-president-trump-withdraws-from-iran-deal/

Sunni-majority United Arab Emirates and Sunni-ruled Bahrain,[186] Sunni Arab states are drawing closer to Israel! Hostility with Iran is being met with more peaceful relations between Israel and Sunni-led nations.

This could, in turn, lead to the short period of peace and security that Israel will enjoy under a covenant with the Antichrist.[187] It is possible that the Gog-Magog debacle in the Iranian-Russian invasion of the Holy Land would have created massive geopolitical vacuum in the Middle East and Europe to clear the way for the rise of the Antichrist. This will be further discussed in Chapter 8.

On the topic of end-time prophecies: Does the rise of radical Islam have anything to do with Bible prophecies about Babylon—in particular the end-time prophecies in Revelation chapters 17–18?

As stated at the outset of this chapter, one of the plausible scenarios from *Proteus: Insights from 2020* foresees a "Saudi Arabian coup"[188] in which "[t]he Saudi Royal Family was overthrown."[189] Given present-day Middle East geopolitics, this might not take place until the period of tribulation immediately before Christ returns (*covered in Chapter 8*).

Babylon the Great Harlot

In terms of What Might Happen After This for the Middle East, Revelation chapters 17 and 18 refer to the judgment and demise of a woman named "Babylon." Revelation 17:5 calls her "Babylon the great, the mother of harlots and the abominations of the earth" (KJV). Traditionally, evangelical commentators believed that "Babylon" is Rome and Babylon's harlotry represents Roman Catholicism. Alternatively, some named the

---

[186] See for example Hassan Rouhani, 2018 May 9, "World leaders react to US withdrawal from Iranian nuclear deal," https://www.aljazeera.com/news/2018/05/world-leaders-react-withdrawal-iranian-nuclear-deal-180508184130931.html

[187] Daniel 9:27, discussed in Chapter 8 of the present book

[188] *Proteus: Insights from 2020*, 2000 Copernicus Institute, Appendix F, page F-xii

[189] *Proteus: Insights from 2020*, 2000 Copernicus Institute, Appendix F, page F-xvi

US as the Babylon of the end times. For the last few decades, this principal author disagreed with each of those interpretations.

The Old and New Testaments of the Bible refer to Babylon more than 280 times. Neither Rome/Roman Catholicism nor the US appear to fit into prophecies about Babylon—including the above-noted prophecy in Revelations 17 and 18. Instead, the prophecies seem to apply to a radical Islamic-based entity. Following are seven sets of passages:

1. Babylon will rule over multitudes:

   - Revelation 17:1—"I will show you the judgment of the great harlot who sits on many waters." (NASB)
   - 17:15—"The waters ... where the harlot sits, are peoples and multitudes and nations and tongues." (NASB)
   - 17:18—"The woman whom you saw is the great city, which reigns over the kings of the earth." (NASB)

These passages predict that this great prostitute at the end time will rule over multitudes of nations, people of various languages, and other kings. As noted in Chapter 2, the US's influence is more likely to wane than to increase. And while Roman Catholicism has experienced revivals here and there, many would agree that in the early twenty-first century, Islam is outpacing Catholicism's worldwide growth.[190] As radical Islamic-based groups expand their geopolitical spheres of influence, they are more likely to satisfy these prophecies than Rome/Roman Catholicism or the US, which are declining in influence.

---

[190] See for example Michael Lipka and Conrad Hackett, 2017 April 6, "Why Muslims are the world's fastest-growing religious group," www.pewresearch.org/fact-tank/2017/04/06/why-muslims-are-the-worlds-fastest-growing-religious-group/

Tricia Escobedo, 2017 March 17, The world's fastest growing religion? Islam https://www.cnn.com/2017/03/16/world/islam-fastest-growing-religion-trnd/index.html

Philip Jenkins, 2012 November, "The World's Fastest Growing Religion," https://www.catholiceducation.org/en/controversy/common-misconceptions/the-world-s-fastest-growing-religion.html

2. The kings of the earth collude immorally with Babylon:

- Revelation 17:2 refers to Babylon as the great harlot "with whom the kings of the earth committed acts of immorality...." (NASB)

Collusion with kings indicates that Babylon is not only a religious power but also a political power on this earth. Sure enough, Islam and radical Islamic groups are already a political influence.

3. Babylon causes drunkenness and madness:

- Revelation 17:2—"Those who dwell on the earth were made drunk with the wine of her immorality." (NASB)
- Jeremiah 51:7—"Babylon has been a golden cup in the hand of the LORD, Intoxicating all the earth. The nations have drunk of her wine; Therefore the nations are going mad." (NASB)

The wine of Babylon's adultery leads to confusion, madness, and intoxication. Although the Roman Catholic Church has committed its share of immorality, it still vaguely points to the God of the Bible. And although US leadership has strayed from the country's founding Christian principles, Chapter 2 indicates that leaders still pay respect to Christianity. But the Islamic fallacy of being the truth revealed by Allah confuses people, fetters their cognition, and impairs their judgment— like the effects of intoxication. Islam and its radical forms continue to captivate and lure people from around the world—with corresponding potential for chaos and madness.

4. Babylon is clothed with nobility, but something sinister could lurk beneath.

- Revelation 17:4—"The woman was clothed in purple and scarlet." (NASB)

- 18:16—"'Woe, woe, the great city, she who was clothed in fine linen and purple and scarlet." (NASB)

In the Bible, purple is a color worn by royalty and associated with nobility and wealth.[191] Scarlet had various symbolic meanings, but in their original Greek, these passages use the word κόκκινον ("KO-keeno"). Greek translations of the Old Testament use the same word for:

- a colour that God chose for constructing his tabernacle (blue, purple, and scarlet [κόκκινον])[192]
- describing sin in Isaiah 1:18—"Though your sins are as scarlet [κόκκινον], They will be as white as snow."
- allure in Song of Songs 4:3 ("Your lips are like a scarlet [κόκκινον] thread.")

The scarlet could also emphasize Babylon's royal appearance; in the ancient world, deep scarlet or crimson could also be made using the same ingredients as purple dye.[193]

Notably, Babylon's scarlet (κόκκινον) is different from the original Greek word used for the "red" war-horse in Revelation 6:4 (πυρρός, "pee-rose"). Perhaps Babylon will be clothed in nobility and allure, while something sinister lurks beneath. Radical Islam could fit that profile as it claims to fight for a righteous, noble cause—using destructive means.

5. Babylon is adorned with wealth and beautiful things:

- Revelation 17:4—"The woman was ... adorned with gold and precious stones and pearls." (NASB)

---

[191] See for example Strong's Concordance, "porphurous," available at biblehub.com/str/greek/4210.htm

[192] See for example Exodus 25:4, 28:5, 31:4, 35:6, 35:23, and 35:25

[193] See for example Strong's Concordance, "porphura," available at biblehub.com/str/greek/4209.htm

- 18:16—"'Woe, woe, the great city, she who was...adorned with gold and precious stones and pearls." (NASB)

In addition to her noble appearance, Babylon will likely accumulate wealth—and show it off. As radical Islamic entities continue to gain influence among states like Saudi Arabia, the United Arab Emirates, and Qatar, it is not difficult to imagine them impressing people through dazzling displays of wealth.

6. Babylon will have an unquenchable thirst for persecuting Christians:

- Revelation 17:6—"And I saw the woman drunk with the blood of the saints, and with the blood of the witnesses of Jesus." (NASB)

The woman (Babylon) not only consumes the blood of believers, but consumes so much that she becomes drunk. She surrenders control in killing believers on a large scale. That description does not fit the Roman Catholic Church or the US, but it certainly fits radical Islamic-based groups who seek to eliminate 'infidels.'

7. Babylon will be a powerful place (until her eventual demise):

- Revelation 18:9–10 describe Babylon's future demise, but the verses also point out her former power: "Woe, woe, the great city, Babylon, the strong city!" (NASB)

Through a combination of state support and grassroots support, radical Islamic-based entities are likely to strengthen their grip of power in the Middle East and other parts of the world. It is possible that at some point, these entities will become too powerful for other global powers to dislodge, especially with the US's decisive withdrawal from the Middle East.

In addition to Revelations 17 and 18, radical Islamic-based entities also fit into other end-time prophecies. For example:

Revelation 20:4 states: "And I saw the souls of those who had been beheaded because of their testimony of Jesus and because of the word of God" (NASB). Wherever radical Islamic entities go, they will despise Christians and others who refuse to accept their particular version of Islam. Such hatred will drive the radicals to behead people, violate women, and confiscate possessions as the spoils of jihad.

Revelation 6:9–10 states: "I saw underneath the altar the souls of those who had been slain because of the word of God….'How long, O Lord, holy and true, will You refrain from judging and avenging our blood on those who dwell on the earth?'" (NASB). It is not difficult to imagine what is described here happening to Christians and other 'infidels' wherever radical Islamic-based entities hold power.

Seen in the biblical context, the armed conflict in Syria is more than an internal struggle over the rule of President Bashar al-Assad; it is an early manifestation of the end-times conflicts that the Bible foresees leading to Gog-Magog war, the rise of The Great Harlot and Armageddon for the Middle East, prior to Christ's return. The important thing is that we rest assured that God is in control of history, and He is coming back soon! Amen. Come, Lord Jesus!

CHAPTER 6

THE IRON AND CLAY MIXTURE BOMBSHELL

Daniel's Vision of a Statue

In June 2018, the world witnessed the bombshell summit between US President Trump and North Korean leader Kim Jong Un in Singapore. What does this unpredecented meeting have to do with What Might Take Place After This?

For the last few centuries, many theologians and Bible expositors have expounded on Daniel chapter 2, the dream of Nebuchadnezzar, king of Babylon. The king saw a colossal statue with a head of gold, arms and chest of silver, belly and thighs of bronze, legs of iron, and feet of mingled iron and clay. Daniel explained to the king that the statue represented four successive kingdoms beginning with Babylon. Daniel described how the King's dream unfolded:

34 "You continued looking until a stone was cut out without hands, and it struck the statue on its feet of iron and clay and crushed them. 35 "Then the iron, the clay, the bronze, the silver and the gold were crushed all at the same time and became like

chaff from the summer threshing floors; and the wind carried them away so that not a trace of them was found. But the stone that struck the statue became a great mountain and filled the whole earth. (NASB)

Many agree on which empires are represented in the statue: Babylon (the head of gold); Medo-Persia (the chest and arms of silver); Greece (the belly and thighs/hips of brass); and Rome (the legs of iron).[194] But there is less consensus in interpreting the feet of mingled (mixed) iron and clay. Some have tried to identify various periods in European history as the clay-and-iron feet; others claim the feet represent the divided Eastern and Western divisions of Rome, supposedly having been 'conquered' by Christianity. Still others believe that the clay-and-iron empire is yet to come: the kingdom of the Antichrist will be a 'Revived Roman Empire.' The latter interpretation proposes that the Roman Empire in some form will be revived and the toes represent a ten-king coalition that has yet to materialize.

In the early 1980s, as this principal author was crisscrossing much of Western Europe representing Canada in numerous North Atlantic Treaty Organization (NATO) meetings, he spent much of his leisure time thinking about Biblical end-time prophecies. If we believed that the statue's feet and toes represent the Revived Roman Empire, then we should probably believe that this empire will extend beyond the Western European nations belonging to NATO. But back in the early 1980s, it was almost unthinkable that a Revived Roman Empire would go beyond the national boundaries of Western Europe to include Eastern European nations, which were under the Soviet Union's powerful grip.

---

[194] See for example "The Dream of a Great Statue," http://www.teachinghearts.org/dre17hdan02.html

Mikhail Gorbachev and the Glasnost

In March 1985 at the age of fifty-four, Mikhail Gorbachev was elected general secretary (party leader) of the Communist Party. It was clear that he was pushing for radical change including an unprecedented peaceful offensive in Europe. Initially, Europeans—especially the youths—were at odds with US President Ronald Reagan's hardline policy against the "evil empire."[195] Reagan had been pressing for the deployment of Pershing missiles to the Soviet Union's doorstep. During those years, this principal author travelled frequently to NATO headquarters in Brussels, Belgium, and often had to go to the Canadian Forces military base in southern Germany to catch military flights back to Canada. At the time, Allied (NATO) military bases in Europe—especially Germany— were always on high alert; they were intensely guarded by armed military person-nel standing behind heavily-fortified gates. In Brussels, our motorcades going between our hotels and NATO headquarters were instructed to vary their daily routes so as to lessen the risk that hostile parties could plan an attack based on a predictable schedule.

This principal author saw how much the Germans were excited with Gorbachev's ascendance and his policy of Glasnost (meaning 'open-ness').[196] But as the Soviet Union launched the Glasnost, this principal author, being familiar with pre-1980s disparities in living standards and opportunities for livelihood between Taiwan and mainland China, started thinking about Glasnost's ultimate domestic impact on the Soviet Union and its Warsaw Pact allies. Would Glasnost ultimately backfire in rattling the core foundation of its iron-fisted domestic policy within the Soviet and Warsaw Pact nations?

---

[195] Speech by President Reagan, 1983 March 8, retrieved from http://voicesof democracy.umd.edu/reagan-evil-empire-speech-text/

[196] See for example "The Gorbachev era: perestroika and glasnost," https://www.britannica.com/place/Russia/The-Gorbachev-era-perestroika-and-glasnost

Two Opposing Camps of the Iron and the Clay

In Daniel 2:41, Daniel interprets part of King Nebuchadnezzar's dream: "You saw the feet and toes, partly of potter's clay and partly of iron, it will be a divided kingdom" (NASB). Later in verse 2:43, Daniel mentions "the iron mixed with common clay" (NASB).

The Cold War era was not the first time that history saw two opposing camps of nations; for example, loyalty in an alliance system pulled countries onto different fronts during World War I. But the Cold War era saw opposing camps based on fundamental differences in ideology and political systems. One side featured an autocratic 'iron curtain' system, and the other side featured a democratic system that could be molded like clay. Nations were divided along the lines of iron versus clay; East and West Germany, Eastern and Western Europe, North and South Vietnam, North and South Korea, and China versus Taiwan.

Before the collapse of the Eastern European communist regime, few would have drawn a connection to the vision of iron and clay in the book of Daniel. Few would have interpreted the iron and clay as representations of opposing political systems. Even fewer would have interpreted the subsequently-mixed iron and clay to mean that nations with distinctive political systems would one day be mixed together.

The German Unification Bombshell

But those ideas lingered in this principal author's mind. And after the collapse of South Vietnam in 1975 despite the US's military and financial support, he started considering the possibility of unification in Germany, Europe, China, and Korea.

In the spring of 1987, he had the honour of welcoming to Ottawa, Canada, his distinguished technical consultant, Dr. William Widnall, former director, Apollo Guidance, Navigation, and Control Program; accompanied by his even more distinguished wife Dr. Sheila Widnall, who was at that time the associate provost of the Massachusetts Institute of Technology (MIT).

Several years later, when Bill Clinton became the US president, Dr. Sheila Widnall was nominated as the secretary of the US Air Force. Hearing this in the news, this principal author called her at her home to congratulate her. She said that initially President Clinton asked her to serve as the director of NASA, but that she declined and the president called back asking her what position she would be interested in. She told the president that if she were offered the position of the secretary of the Air Force, then she would seriously consider it. As her nomination was confirmed, I called Dr. William Widnall to congratulate him and his wife. Dr. William Widnall told me that when he phoned his mother in-law to celebrate his wife's confirmed appointment, his mother in-law was bewildered that her daughter could serve as a secretary of the US Air Force without knowing how to type. It seemed she did not quite appreciate that her daughter had become the first woman to lead an entire branch of the US armed forces.

During this distinguished couple's visit, this principal author and his wife took them out for a dinner. Toward the end of the meal, this principal author raised an issue that had been dear to his heart—namely, the possibility that East and West Germany would unify as a nation. To his surprise, his distinguished consultant rapidly dismissed that notion as being impossible given the devastating tally of human casualties during German invasions in the two world wars; if the Soviet Union (USSR) had any political or military influence in the world, there is no way that the Soviet Union would ever allow Germany to unify as a nation again, becoming a fresh threat to the lives of Soviet citizens. Dr. Widnall was clearly well versed in the potential consequences of German reunification, so the discussion moved to other topics.

Nonetheless, this principal author shared his thoughts of German reunification when invited to write an article for *Proclaim Magazine*—as mentioned earlier, a publication of Chinese Christian Mission. The article was prepared in 1988 and published in May 1989.

On 9 November 1989, the world was stunned to see the sudden collapse of the Berlin Wall, followed in 1991 by the dissolution of the Warsaw Pact and the total collapse of the Soviet Union without one shot being fired in anger.

Further regarding this 'mixture of iron and clay': there was previously a well-defined autocratic communist system of government with a centralized planning economic management system, which stood in contrast to a democratic system of government with a capitalist market economy. This is no longer the case in China or in Vietnam. After Vietnam unified under the communist party leadership, Vietnam liberalized its economy and adopted a market economy. Likewise, under the leadership of Deng Xiao Ping, China revamped its central planning economy and started to experiment with a market economy. Though debates persist regarding the true extent of its market system,[197] China has now embraced capitalistic characteristics.

Conversely, Western democracies have seen exceptional central-government intervention in their own capitalistic free markets. In response to the international economic crisis of 2008, which was prompted by the US sub-prime mortgage crisis, the US federal government issued precedent-setting bailouts to the automotive industry and banking institutions.

The Unification of China and Taiwan Bombshell

There is no doubt that China and Taiwan will eventually be unified. Mainland China's nationalist Republic of China (RoC) government was established in 1912 while Taiwan was under Japan's control. China got Taiwan back from Japan in 1945, but the nationalists fled to Taiwan in 1949 after losing a civil war with the Communists. Taiwan maintains

---

[197] See for example the summaries at https://forbes.com/sites/douglasbulloch/2017/12/08/china-is-not-a-market-economy-and-the-wto-wont-survive-recognising-it-as-such/ and https://www.forbes.com/sites/sarahsu/2017/12/04/u-s-rejection-of-china-market-economy-status-will-damage-trade-relations/

the RoC name. China's Communist-led government regards Taiwan as a breakaway province which China will not allow to secede from the mainland. As of January 2018, only eighteen countries and the Vatican recognize Taiwan as a sovereign nation.[198] In 2017, Taiwan's annual military budget was $10.5 billion US dollars and China's annual military budget was $210 billion US dollars. Even with help from the US, Taiwan cannot indefinitely resist reunification with China.

In February 2018, *The American Conservative* magazine presented the question: "Will the US Go to War With China Over Taiwan?"[199] The article was subtitled: "It's time to rethink our defense commitments. Risking a catastrophic conflict is too great a price for Taiwanese independence." The risk calculation was explained as follows:

[In recent years,] Beijing has invested hundreds of billions of dollars in military modernization efforts, especially to develop antiship missiles and other "access denial" systems. Today, a US intervention to save Taiwan would still likely succeed, but it would be far more perilous and come at a much greater cost in blood and treasure. In another few years, prospects for success will be even more uncertain.

The United States needs to reassess the TRA [1979 Taiwan Relations Act] and separate the obligations it contains. Washington should continue to sell arms to Taiwan, despite Beijing's predictable, chronic protests. Such sales give the Taiwanese the option to continue resisting the PRC's demands for steps towards reunification, if they wish to incur the attendant risk. However, US leaders should also make it clear that

---

[198] See for example Austin Ramzy, 2018 May 1, "Taiwan's Diplomatic Isolation Increases as Dominican Republic Recognizes China," https://www.nytimes.com/2018/05/01/world/asia/taiwan-dominican-republic-recognize.html

[199] Ted Galen Carpenter, 2018 February 20, "Will the US Go to War With China Over Taiwan?" www.theamericanconservative.com/articles/will-the-u-s-go-to-war-with-china-over-taiwan/
Used by permission of The American Conservative together with the author.

Taiwan is on its own and alter the TRA's language to remove any implied defense commitment. As fond as we might be of a vibrant, democratic Taiwan, risking a catastrophic war with China is far too great a price to pay to preserve the island's de facto independence.

In November 2018, the New York Times reported: *"Taiwan's President Quits as Party Chief After Stinging Losses in Local Races."*[200] *This news report highlighted:*

> The president of Taiwan resigned as leader of her party Saturday night after it suffered stunning local election defeats to the opposition Kuomintang, which favors closer ties with China.
>
> Opposition Kuomintang mayoral candidates won in Taiwan's three largest cities — New Taipei City, Taichung and Kaohsiung. The Kaohsiung contest was especially stinging for the D.P.P., which has held the mayor's office for 20 years and considered the southern city a political stronghold.

Losing the Kaoshiung mayoral race to the DPP was a significant defeat for Taiwan's pro-independent movement,since Kaoshing is the most entrenched stronghold for the independence in Taiwan. Until then, the DPP had held the city without any interruption for 20 years.

On the same day, the *Washington Post* reported that the "Taiwanese reject gay marriage, new Olympic name. "[201]

> Voters in Taiwan have approved a referendum opposing same-sex marriage while rejecting a proposal to change the name of its Olympic team to Taiwan from the current Chinese Taipei.

---

[200] **https://www.nytimes.com/2018/11/24/world/asia/taiwan-election-results.html**

[201] https://www.washingtonpost.com/world/asia_pacific/the-latest-china-says-taiwan-vote-a-desire-for-better-ties/2018/11/24/105d9d8c-f04c-11e8-8b47-bd0 975fd6199_story.html?noredirect=on&utm_term=.a0f5b9239bcd

The referendums were among 10 on the ballot during island-wide city mayoral elections Saturday that dealt a major setback to President Tsai Ing-wen's independence-leaning party.

The proposal to use the name Taiwan at future international sports events was opposed by China, which considers Taiwan a part of its territory. It was seen as a test of support for independence.

The results of this local election and more importantly the overwhelming rejection of the Referendum on changing the name to Taiwan, show the diminishing support for Taiwan independence by Taiwan voters.

The Unification of North Korea and South Korea Bombshell

And what of a possible reunification between Korean iron and clay? In 1945 at the same time as Japan ceded control over Taiwan, it also ceded control over Korea. The Korean peninsula was divided between a Soviet-occupied northern portion and a US-protected southern portion. North and South remained divided after the Korean War's ceasefire of 1953.

Since 2006 when North Korea conducted its first nuclear test, the international community has applied numerous economic sanctions against the country which North Korea often met with further nuclear tests and threats.[202] Official rhetoric on this matter has been colourful and at times alarming. According to *The New York Times*, North Korean officials have repeatedly warned the US and South Korea against pre-emptive attacks by threatening to respond with a "sea of fire."[203]

---

[202] See for example Eleanor Albert, 2018 January 3, "What to Know About the Sanctions on North Korea," https://www.cfr.org/backgrounder/what-know-about-sanctions-north-korea

[203] See for example Peter Baker and Choe Sang-Hun, 2018 August 8, "Trump Threatens 'Fire and Fury' Against North Korea if It Endangers US," https://www.nytimes.

As recently as August 2017, when North Korea was said to have created a miniaturized nuclear weapon designed to fit inside its missiles, US President Donald J. Trump used "chilling language that evoked the horror of a nuclear exchange":

"North Korea best not make any more threats to the United States," Mr. Trump told reporters…. "They will be met with fire and fury like the world has never seen…. "He [North Korean leader Kim Jong Un] has been very threatening beyond a normal state, and as I said, they will be met with fire and fury, and frankly power the likes of which this world has never seen before."[204]

The New York Times noted the US's lack of success in leveraging China (an ally to North Korea) to get North Korea to change its course:

While Mr. Trump's statement is among the most militant a president has made about North Korea, it may have been aimed as much at Beijing as at Pyongyang. By discussing military options, the administration may be trying to convince China and its president, Xi Jinping, that the status quo is dangerous because it risks war.[205]

On January 1, 2018, North Korean leader "Kim Jong Un warned that the United States should be aware that his country's nuclear forces

---

com/2017/08/08/world/asia/north-korea-un-sanctions-nuclear-missile-united-nations.html

[204] See for example Peter Baker and Choe Sang-Hun, 2018 August 8, "Trump Threatens 'Fire and Fury' Against North Korea if It Endangers US," https://www.nytimes.com/2017/08/08/world/asia/north-korea-un-sanctions-nuclear-missile-united-nations.html

[205] See for example Peter Baker and Choe Sang-Hun, 2018 August 8, "Trump Threatens 'Fire and Fury' Against North Korea if It Endangers US," https://www.nytimes.com/2017/08/08/world/asia/north-korea-un-sanctions-nuclear-missile-united-nations.html

are now a reality, not a threat. But he also struck a conciliatory tone in his New Year's address, wishing success for the Winter Olympics set to begin in the South in February and suggesting the North may send a delegation to participate."[206] Soon after, on January 17, 2018, South Korea came out with a bombshell announcement of diplomatic breakthrough following days of talks between the two countries. North and South Korean athletes would march together at the Winter Olympics opening ceremony under a unified flag.[207]

In February 2018, the US administration affirmed its 100 percent commitment to "the permanent denuclearization of the Korean Peninsula."[208] Some believed that the administration was considering military action if North Korea succeeded in building a nuclear missile capable of hitting the US.[209] But shortly thereafter, in March 2018, South Korea's national security advisor relayed the bombshell that North Korean leader Kim Jong Un wished to meet with President Trump regarding denuclearization, and that President Trump had agreed to meet by May 2018.[210] The following month, April 2018, US officials stated that North Korean officials directly informed the US of their willingness to discuss denuclearization when President Trump met with Kim Jong

---

[206] CBS/Associated Press, 2018 January 1, "Kim Jong Un warns "button for nuclear weapons is on my table"" https://www.cbsnews.com/news/kim-jong-un-north-korea-completed-nuclear-forces/

[207] See for example Choe Sang-Hun, 2018 January 17, "North and South Korean Teams to March as One at Olympics," https://www.nytimes.com/2018/01/17/world/asia/north-south-korea-olympics.html

[208] 2018 February 26, "Press Briefing by Press Secretary Sarah Sanders," https://www.whitehouse.gov/briefings-statements/press-briefing-press-secretary-sarah-sanders-022618/

[209] Jim Sciutto and Dana Bash, 2018 March 1, "Nuclear missile threat a 'red line' for Trump on North Korea," https://www.cnn.com/2018/03/01/politics/north-korea-trump-nuclear-missile-threat-red-line/index.html

[210] 2018 March 8, "Remarks by Republic of Korea National Security Advisor Chung Eui-Yong," https://www.whitehouse.gov/briefings-statements/remarks-republic-korea-national-security-advisor-chung-eui-yong/

Un.[211] That would be the first meeting between a sitting US president and a North Korean leader—and thus a gamble for both parties.

Later in the same month, April 2018, North Korean leader Kim Jong Un shockingly announced during the third plenary meeting of the Seventh Central Committee of the Workers' Party of Korea (WPK) in Pyongyang that "from 21 April, North Korea will stop nuclear tests and launches of intercontinental ballistic missiles." Cessation of testing does not, however, equate to denuclearization; rather North Korea claims that they no longer need to conduct tests because they have completed their nuclear product.[212]

Nonetheless, that double-edged announcement was followed by a historic summit on 27 April 2018 between South Korean President Moon Jae-in and the North Korean leader. At the summit, the two leaders signed the Panmunjom Declaration for Peace, Prosperity and Unification on the Korean Peninsula, which commits the two countries to denuclearization and talks to bring a formal end to conflict.[213] Kim Jong Un stated: "Using one language, one culture, one history South and North Korea will be reunited as one country, thus enjoying everlasting peace and prosperity." And Moon pledged: "There will be no more war on the Korean peninsula."

---

[211] Matt Spetalnick, David Brunnstrom, 2018 April 8, "North Korea tells US it is prepared to discuss denuclearization: source," https://www.reuters.com/article/us-northkorea-missiles-talks/north-korea-tells-u-s-it-is-prepared-to-discuss-denuclearization-source-idUSKBN1HF0WQ

[212] See for example "North Korea missile and nuclear test halt hailed," 2018 April 21, http://www.bbc.com/news/world-asia-43849516
and BBC, "North Korea 'halts missile and nuclear tests', says Kim Jong-un," 2018 April 21, http://www.bbc.com/news/world-asia-43846488
and Bruce Klingner, 2018 April 23, "What Is Kim Jong Un Thinking?" http://nationalinterest.org/feature/what-kim-jong-un-thinking-25523

[213] Reuters Staff, 2018 April 27, "Panmunjom Declaration for Peace, Prosperity and Unification of the Korean Peninsula" https://uk.reuters.com/article/uk-northkorea-southkorea-summit-statemen/panmunjom-declaration-for-peace-prosperity-and-unification-of-the-korean-peninsula-idUKKBN1HY193

The Historic Trump and Kim Summit Bombshells

In June 2018, Trump and Kim Jong Un held an unprecedented meeting in Singapore. The following day, many major news outlets carried an *Associated Press* article stating that the Trump-Kim summit raised cautious hope for peace.[214]

> Many have applauded the recent months of denuclearization diplomacy between North Korea and the US after a year of mounting tension, threats, and name-calling. Hopes for peace on the long-divided Korean Peninsula, however, remained tempered by the many failed attempts in the past.
>
> "The United States and North Korea have been in a state of antagonism for more than half a century," Chinese Foreign Minister Wang Yi said. "Today, that the two countries' highest leaders can sit together and have equal talks, has important and positive meaning, and is creating a new history."
>
> Moon [South Korean President Moon Jae-in] said he "could hardly sleep" in anticipation of the meeting and expressed hope for "complete denuclearization and peace." ... Japanese Prime Minister Shinzo Abe welcomed Kim's written commitment to complete denuclearization in an agreement signed with Trump at the end of their meeting in Singapore.[215]

In July 2018, CNBC reported that "the US is trying to nail down terms with Pyongyang, while 'South Koreans aren't wasting time'":

---

[214] The Associated Press, 2018 June 12, "Trump-Kim talks inspire glee, cautious optimism, skepticism," https://www.apnews.com/b9e68b4341c44fbc818cdfcfb0 f1032f/SOMNIA

[215] 2018 June 12, https://indianexpress.com/article/world/donald-trump-kim-jong-un-north-korea-meeting-singapore-5214537/

In South Korea, the mood is overwhelmingly optimistic as President Moon Jae-in's government pushes for improved ties with its nuclear-armed neighbor.

From sports diplomacy to corporate ventures, Seoul is pulling out all the stops ... as it builds on the positive momentum sparked by April's inter-Korean summit.

Major conglomerates such as Lotte, Hyundai, Hyosung, and KT have announced task forces dedicated to exploring inter-Korean ventures.[216]

Meanwhile the British newspaper *The Independent* reported: "Donald Trump shares gushing letter from Kim Jong-un praising him:"[217]

The note is a follow up to the pair's 12 June [2018] summit in Singapore about ending North Korea's nuclear weapons programme.

Mr Kim had written he "deeply appreciate[s] the energetic and extraordinary efforts by your Excellency Mr. President" during the summit to improve relations between the adversaries.

He also wrote that Pyongyang has "invariable trust and confidence" in Mr Trump and hoped it will "be further strengthened in the future process of taking practical actions".

Mr Trump called the missive "a very nice note" and said "great progress" is being made towards ending North Korea's nuclear programme."

---

[216] Nyshka Chandran, 2018 July 13, "The US is trying to nail down terms with Pyongyang, while 'South Koreans aren't wasting time'," https://www.cnbc.com/2018/07/12/south-korea-increases-engagement-with-north-korea.html

[217] Mythili Sampathkumar, 2018 July 12, "Donald Trump shares gushing letter from Kim Jong-un praising him," https://www.independent.co.uk/news/world/americas/us-politics/trump-kim-jong-un-letter-us-north-korea-nuclear-weapons-twitter-a8444971.html

In September 2018, the Reuters news agency reported that North Korea left nuclear missiles out of a military parade marking the seventieth anniversary of the country's founding:

With no long-range missiles on display, North Korea staged a military parade on Sunday focused on conventional arms, peace and economic development.[218]

According to Reuters, US President Trump interpreted the absence of nuclear missiles as a sign of North Korea's "commitment to denuclearize."

In January 2019, CNN reported that "White House announces second Trump-Kim summit."[219] The announcement came after Trump met with Kim Yong Chol, North Korea's lead negotiator on nuclear talks, for more than 90 minutes in the Oval Office and discussed "denuclearization and a second summit, which will take place near the end of February," according to press secretary Sarah Sanders. CNN also reported that Vice President Mike Pence made it clear this week that the US is still waiting for North Korea to take concrete steps to denuclearize.

So the bombshell of North Korean denuclearization will continue to play out in the coming months or years.

---

[218] Josh Smith, 2018 September 9, "North Korea military parade features floats and flowers, not missiles," https://www.reuters.com/article/us-northkorea-anniversary-military-parad/no-long-range-missiles-north-korea-military-parade-features-floats-and-flowers-idUSKCN1LP045

[219] https://www.cnn.com/2019/01/18/politics/pompeo-kim-yong-chol-north-korea-washington/index.html

Korean Peninsula Bombshell

In September 2018 as the leaders of both Koreas signed the Pyongyang Joint Declaration,[220] CNN reported North and South Korea's commitment to an "era of no war":

> Kim and Moon vowed to bring peace to the Korean Peninsula once and for all, something they first committed to at their April [2018] summit.
>
> "The world is going to see how this divided nation is going to bring about a new future on its own," Kim said to applause from those gathered.

On the same occasion, an editorial published in the British Independent stated: "The future of the Korean peninsula has never looked brighter than it does now."[221]

In December 2018, the *Guardian* reported that "Kim Jong-un vows to meet South Korea's leader frequently in 2019."[222] The article stated:

> North Korea's leader, Kim Jong-un, has vowed in a rare letter to meet the South's president, Moon Jae-in, "frequently" next year to discuss denuclearisation of the Korean peninsula, Moon's office said on Sunday.

---

[220] The full text of the Pyongyang Declaration is available at http://www.koreatimes.co.kr/www/nation/2018/09/103_255848.html

[221] The *Independent*, 2018 September 19, "The future of the Korean peninsula has never looked brighter than it does now," https://www.independent.co.uk/voices/editorials/north-korea-kim-jong-un-president-moon-donald-trump-denuclearisation-a8545286.html

[222] https://www.theguardian.com/world/2018/dec/30/kim-jong-un-vows-to-meet-south-koreas-leader-frequently-in-2019

Moon welcomed the latest message, saying the North's leader had also expressed "active intention to carry out agreements" made in his previous summits with the US and the South, without elaborating further.

"I welcome chairman Kim's intention to solve together the issue of denuclearisation ... by meeting frequently even next year," Moon said in a statement.

Bombshells of Five Iron and Clay Unifications

Moving from the remarkable possibility of a peaceful Korean reunification, it would not be much of a stretch to imagine the unification of China and Taiwan. The respective reunifications of East and West Germany, Eastern and Western Europe, and North and South Vietnam would amount to five mergers of iron and clay. Can these previously-unimaginable unifications be five flukes, purely coincidental applications of Daniel's prophecies from 2,600 years ago? As noted above, four of the five unifications (Germany, Europe, China, and Korea) were specifically foreseen as applications of the mixed iron and clay before the events took place. If these are what Daniel's prophecies had in mind, it would mean that Daniel foresaw these occurrences more than 2,600 years ago. That would be incredible by human standards. But the Bible states that the Lord's word is "firmly fixed in the heavens" (Psalm 119:89, ESV). All these recent geopolitical bombshells are but preludes to a more significant series of events. In Daniel 2, the statue King Nebuchadnezzar's dream meets a dramatic end:

34 "You continued looking until a stone was cut out without hands, and it struck the statue on its feet of iron and clay and crushed them. 35 "Then the iron, the clay, the bronze, the silver and the gold were crushed all at the same time [...] But the

stone that struck the statue became a great mountain and filled the whole earth. (NASB)

Daniel 2:33 and 41–42 state that the iron and clay constituted the statue's "feet" and "toes." If the colossal statue—which stands tall at the beginning of the dream—were to represent human political empires, then the feet and toes would be at the very end of human empires. The mixture of iron and clay would precede the arrival of a rock extracted not by human hands; this would be among the rare Bible prophecies giving us a precise time frame of what will happen on earth leading up to Christ's second coming.

As we hear the hastening footsteps leading to the incredible and near-impossible mixing of iron and clay, we should take heed that Jesus is coming back soon. Amen. Come, Lord Jesus.

CHAPTER 7

THE MIDDLE KINGDOM
BOMBSHELL

Spiritual Bondage in Another Ancient Civilization

In modern times, the most common name for China is *Zhōngguó*, literally translated as Middle Kingdom. China is also called *Zhonghua* (中華 or 中华), *Shenzhou* (神州), and *Huaxia* (華夏 or 华夏). *Han* (漢/汉) and *Tang* (唐) are common names for the dominant Chinese ethnic group.[223] The ultimate source of the Western-language name China is the Chinese word Qin (秦), the name of the dynasty that gradually unified China by 221 BC.

China stands among a tiny handful of nations having both a very ancient civilization and great power in the modern day. This despite suffering a "century of humiliation" at the hands of Western powers and Japan between 1839 and 1949 and other major turmoil such as more than two decades of civil war (1927 to 1949), the decade-long political and social chaos of the Cultural Revolution (1966 to 1976), and student-led protests in Tiananmen Square (1989).

---

[223] China's population includes at least fifty-six different ethnic groups. The Han ethnic group—the one typically associated with the term 'Chinese'—is the most numerous.

China's 5,000 years of civilization comes with a deep-rooted tradition of ancestral worship. Foot binding was another ancient tradition, considered a mark of status and beauty for women and practised for one thousand years until the early twentieth century.

Robert Morrison: I Can't, But I Believe God Can

In September 1807, twenty-five-year-old Robert Morrison boarded a ship for the seven-month voyage from England through the US to the port of Guangzhou in China. He was the first Protestant missionary to China, following God's call to reach the country's 350 million souls with the gospel.

As Morrison stood on the deck of the ship, looking at the teeming crowds on the banks, a shipping agent asked him shortly before their arrival in China: "Do you really think you can influence China's deep tradition of ancestral worship?" For a brief moment Morrison was at a loss for words, and then he replied: "No, sir, I can't, but I believe God can."

When the Bible proclaimed: "God so loved the world that He gave His only begotten Son," God's love must include the Chinese—the world's most numerous people group.

When China went through the turmoil of the Cultural Revolution (1966 to 1976), churches were forcibly closed, many of the Christian leaders were imprisoned and/or killed for their faith, and many others spent years in hard-labour camps. In that era, it would have appeared that all the sacrifice, bloodshed, and labours of love by tens of thousands of missionaries from around the world had gone to waste.

Likewise, the social/ political turmoil of 1989 would have led to the question: 'God, why is it that you do not seem to care?'

"Jesus in Beijing"

In late 2003, David Aikman, former Beijing bureau chief for *Time* magazine, published a book called *"Jesus in Beijing" How Christianity Is Transforming China and Changing the Global Balance of Power*.[224] According to a review in the May/June 2004 issue of *Foreign Affairs* magazine:[225]

> He [Aikman] estimates that "Christian believers in China, both Catholic and Protestant, may be closer to 80 million than the official combined Catholic-Protestant figure of 21 million" and that "it is possible that Christians will constitute 20 to 30 percent of China's population within three decades."

A review by a Global China Center academic stated:[226]

> According to Aikman, we are talking not just about an incredible increase in the number of Chinese Christians in the past fifty years (from one or two million to more than 70 million), but what might become a fundamental shift in world power alignments.
>
> In other words, the spread of a vibrant Christian faith throughout all echelons of society could produce a "critical mass" of believers who would impact both domestic and foreign policy. Specifically, Evangelical Christians could tilt their

---

[224] David Aikman, 2003, *Jesus in Beijing: How Christianity Is Transforming China and Changing the Global Balance of Power* (Regnery Publishing)

[225] Lucian W. Pye, 2004 May/June issue https://www.foreignaffairs.com/reviews/capsule-review/2004-05-01/jesus-beijing-how-christianity-transforming-china-and-changing

[226] Dr. G. Wright Doyle, 2003 February 19, http://www.globalchinacenter.org/analysis/christianity-in-china/jesus-in-beijing-how-christianity-is-transforming-china-and-changing-the-global-balance-of-power.php

nation towards America in the global conflict between Islam and the West.

God Used Mao to Remove Deeply-Ingrained Bondage

Two paradigm shifts deserve more attention than what they received in Aikman's book:

Firstly, the Cultural Revolution (1966–1976) had the significant impact of removing Chinese people in China from five thousand years of bondage to ancestral worship. Communist leader Mao Zedung—as part of his enormous effort to remove four old traditions (old customs, culture, habits, and ideas)—swept away this deep-rooted bondage of ancestral worship that long prevented Chinese people from opening their hearts to the gospel.

Whether he knew it or not, Robert Morrison was describing exactly this type of divine intervention when he professed faith that "God can" influence the Chinese tradition of ancestral worship. God effectively used Mao to remove the 5,000-year-old bondage of ancestral worship. In Chapter 4, we mentioned Isaiah 45:1 referring to Cyrus as God's anointed:

"Thus says the LORD to Cyrus His anointed, Whom I have taken by the right hand ... (NASB)." Usually the phrase "the anointed" refers to the Messiah, the King of the Jews. But in this instance, Cyrus was anointed in the sense of being raised up and qualified by divine counsel (God's will), to perform God's good pleasure."[227]

Defining "the anointed" in this particular sense, we could be so bold as to view Chairman Mao as another of God's anointed—raised up and qualified to break through the 5,000-year-old bondage of ancestral worship in China. Among Chinese populations the world over, Chinese people raised in China are now the least bound to ancestral worship

---

[227] See for example Joseph Benson and Matthew Henry's commentaries, retrieved from http://biblehub.com/commentaries/isaiah/45-1.htm

and the most receptive to the gospel. This important paradigm shift has made Christianity spread like wildfire across mainland China.

Secondly, the 1989 student-led protests in favour of political and economic reform. Chinese intellectuals have traditionally been the champions and guardians of Chinese culture and nationalism. Therefore they have been most resistant to the gospel propagated by 'foreign devils.' As they saw the 1989 bloodshed in Tiananmen Square,[228] the Chinese intelligentsia who cared for the nation's wellbeing were overcome with such despair that they embraced a paradigm shift en masse, opening their minds to Christ.

As a result of these two momentous paradigm shifts, the growth rate of the Chinese church since 1949 more than doubled the growth rate of Christianity from the time when Jesus ascended into the Heaven until the year 311 when Constantine mandated that the gospel be tolerated. The result of these two paradigm shifts will be elaborated later in the context of the Chinese Christian Growth Bombshell.

God Loves the Chinese

After the 1989 student-led protests, many knowledgeable political and economic pundits thought that China would soon collapse; many books were written predicting the impending collapse of China's economy and the nation itself. This principal author intentionally wrote a Chinese-language article titled "God loves the Chinese," published in *Chinese Christian Magazine* in January 1994.

The article pointed out that China could continue growing rapidly because the following seven pillars of support were in place:

1. Hong Kong's international trade, finance and business management network, and experience as well as capability in light industry;

---

[228] See for example "Tiananmen Square Incident," last updated 2018 April 20, retrieved from https://www.britannica.com/event/Tiananmen-Square-incident

2. Singapore's international trade and financial expertise and networks;

3. Taiwan's commercial trading network, experience and high technology capability, as well as its experiments with democracy leading up to the 1990s;

4. Ample Chinese scientific and technical talents in North America;

5. China's abundant supply of low-cost labour;

6. China's abundant supply of natural resources; and

7. Large and broadly-available markets.

China's immense progress since 1989 has proven this principal author's analysis to be more trustworthy than the predictions of well-known pundits who expected China's impending collapse.

China Is a Sleeping Giant

French Emperor Napoléon Bonaparte is credited with stating in the year 1803: "China is a sleeping giant. Let her sleep! For when she wakes, she will shake the world."[229] The statement obtained a new lease on life in the context of China's remarkable growth since the death of Mao in 1976. When China began making reforms and opening their policies forty years ago, it had no blueprint. The Chinese were simply pragmatic and willing to experiment, a process that Mao's successor Deng Xiaoping described as "crossing the river by feeling the stones." China went from extreme poverty forty years ago to becoming the second-largest economy today, possessing the world's largest foreign reserves standing at more than three trillion US dollars. China's publicly-declared military spending (land, sea, and air) has been growing 8 to 12 percent annually. It is quickly becoming one of the most important sources of foreign

---

[229] The original French language describes China as a lion, not a giant : « La Chine est un lion endormi qui fera trembler le monde lorsqu'il s'éveillera. »

investment. All of these factors point in the same direction: China is well on its way to take away the US's global leader status.

Thomas Friedman, foreign affairs columnist for *The New York Times*, once wrote:[230]

> When I was growing up, my parents used to say to me: "Finish your dinner—people in China are starving." I, by contrast, find myself wanting to say to my daughters: "Finish your home-work—people in China and India are starving for your job."

Possible Chinese Century

In January 2015, *Vanity Fair* published an article by Nobel Prize-winner Joseph E. Stiglitz entitled: "The Chinese Century."[231] Stiglitz wrote:

> 2014 was the last year in which the United States could claim to be the world's largest economic power. China enters 2015 in the top position, where it will likely remain for a very long time, if not forever. In doing so, it returns to the position it held through most of human history.

This assessment was based on "purchasing-power parities," which enable the comparison of incomes in various countries. Stiglitz cautioned: "These shouldn't be taken as precise numbers, but they do provide a good basis for assessing the relative size of different economies.

---

[230] Thomas L. Friedman, 2004 June 24 "Doing Our Homework," https://www.nytimes.com/2004/06/24/opinion/doing-our-homework.html

[231] Joseph E. Stiglitz, 2015, "The Chinese Century," in *Vanity Fair*, www.vanityfair.com/news/2015/01/china-worlds-largest-economy

Warren Buffett's View of China

In early 2018, the tremendously-successful investor Warren Buffett spoke to Yahoo—Finance's editor-in-chief Andy Serwer about China's economic miracle and how it affects the US[232] Buffett spoke highly of China's economic growth and expressed optimism about its future.

> [Buffett said,] "What they've done in the last 50 or 60 years is a total economic miracle ...they have found a secret sauce for themselves...."
>
> China's state capitalism emphasizes economic growth and social stability, with tight control over domestic politics and information. Since the economic reform in 1978, China has grown at a staggering pace of 9.5% per year and has become the world's second largest economy. In the past five years, China's GDP growth has slowed down but still achieved an increase of 6.9% last year, dwarfing America's 2.3% increase.

In December 2017, the London-based Center for Economics and Business Research[233] forecasted that China will likely overtake the US as the world's largest economy by 2032. Buffett thinks it will take much longer for China to catch up, but "he acknowledges the potential since China's population is almost four times greater than the US. 'The main thing you have to do is unleash the potential of your people.'"[234]

---

[232] Krystal Hu, 2018 April 29, "Warren Buffett: China has 'found a secret sauce for themselves'," retrieved from https://finance.yahoo.com/news/warren-buffett-china-found-secret-sauce-183809314.html

[233] The Yahoo! Finance article refers to Fergal O'Brien, 2017 December 25, "China to Overtake US Economy by 2032 as Asian Might Builds," retrieved from https://www.bloomberg.com/news/articles/2017-12-26/china-to-overtake-u-s-economy-by-2032-as-asian-might-builds.
   The Centre's original World Economic League Table 2018, released on December 26, 2017, is available from https://cebr.com/welt-2018/

[234] Krystal Hu, 2018 April 29, "Warren Buffett: China has 'found a secret sauce for themselves'," retrieved from https://finance.yahoo.com/news/warren-buffett-china-found-secret-sauce-183809314.html

Buffett also adopted a global perspective

"If you postulate two kinds of worlds 50 years from now, and one is where the United States is still doing far better than a good many of the world's people, or you postulate something where everybody is making a lot of progress, I think you've gotta choose the second world." said Buffett. "We should welcome a more prosperous world, including China."

China's "Dangerous" Credit-Based Economic Growth

Not long before Buffett's comments, however, in August 2017 the IMF (International Monetary Fund)[235] reportedly warned China over its "dangerous" credit-based economic growth. According to the British newspaper *The Guardian*,[236] the IMF said China's pursuit of "growth at any cost" risks a "sharp slowdown or financial crisis":

While the IMF increased its forecast for Chinese expansion in 2017 from 6.2% to 6.7%, it stressed that this was the result of the authorities in Beijing putting a higher priority on hitting a growth target than on the quality of the economic output.

The Chinese government has pledged to double the size of the economy between 2010 and 2020 and has been prepared to see non-financial sector debt rise rapidly in order to achieve its aim. Total debt has quadrupled since the financial crisis to stand at $28tn (£22tn) at the end of last year.

---

[235] The IMF is made up of 189 countries "working to foster global monetary cooperation, secure financial stability, facilitate international trade, ..." See for example "About the IMF," www.imf.org/en/About

[236] Larry Elliott, 2017 August 15, "IMF warns China over 'dangerous' growth in debt," https://www.theguardian.com/business/2017/aug/15/imf-warns-china-debt-slowdown-financial-crisis

China's Systemic Financial Risks

Similarly, leading up to November 2017 the governor of China's central bank "issued a series of straightforward warnings" about the risks in China's financial sector. As reported by *The Diplomat* magazine:[237]

> [Recently,] Zhou [governor of the People's Bank of China] urged China to beware of "systemic financial risks" and argued that deepened reform and opening up are the key measures to pro-actively control such risks in China's financial sector.

> In terms of systemic risks, his rhetorics[*sic*] were unusually harsh. Zhou said:

> "China's financial sector is and will be in a period with high risks that are easily triggered. Under pressure from multiple factors at home and abroad, the risks are multiple, broad, hidden, complex, sudden, contagious, and hazardous. The structural unbalance is salient; law-breaking and disorders are rampant; latent risks are accumulating; [and the financial system's] vul-nerability is obviously increasing. [China] should prevent both the "black swan" events [random and unexpected events] and the "gray rhino" risks [a threat that everyone sees coming but fails to address]."

> In his latest article, Zhou elaborated on the top three financial risks China is faced with: the high-leveraging ratio and liquidity in macrofinance; the credit risk in microfinance; and cross-market and cross-regional shadow banking together with financial crime.

---

[237] Charlotte Gao, 2017 November 9, "China's Central Bank Governor Warns About Financial Risks—Again," https://thediplomat.com/2017/11/chinas-central-bank-governor-warns-about-financial-risks-again/

China Local Governments' Hidden Debt

In October 2018, Reuters news service carried an S&P Global Ratings report that "Off-balance-sheet borrowings by Chinese local governments could be as high as 40 trillion yuan ($5.78 trillion) and amount to "a debt iceberg with titanic credit risks:"[238]

> Concerns about debt levels in China, particularly local borrowing, are on the rise as the economy cools amid deepening trade frictions with the United States.
>
> ...China is likely to require a decade or more to address its hidden local government debt, S&P said.

China's Possible Roles at the End Time

Whatever the future course of China's economy, many students of Bible prophecy think that China might have a role to play during the end-times.

Of particular interest is Revelation 16:12–16, an end-times passage that could refer to China:

> 12 And the sixth angel poured out his vial upon the great river Euphrates; and the water thereof was dried up, that the way of the kings of the east might be prepared. 13 And I saw three unclean spirits... 14 For they are the spirits of devils, working miracles, which go forth unto the kings of the earth and of the whole world, to gather them to the battle of that great day of God Almighty. ... 16 And he gathered them together into a place called in the Hebrew tongue Armageddon. (KJV)

[238] https://www.reuters.com/article/us-china-economy-debt/china-local-governments-hidden-debt-could-total-58-trillion-sp-idUSKCN1MQ0JH

This passage predicts a climactic conflict known as the Battle of Armageddon. At this point, the earth has experienced a period of tribulation. The Euphrates River will have dried up, allowing the "kings of the east" (verse 12) to march toward Israel. The Euphrates River originates in eastern Turkey, flowing southeast through Syria and Iraq, merging with the Tigris River and emptying into the Persian Gulf. Countries that are geographically east of the Euphrates (countries whose armies could march toward Israel if the river were dried up) include northeastern Syria, northeastern Iraq, Iran, Afghanistan, Pakistan, India, and China among others.

Kings of the East

Many interpret the "kings of the east" to mean China. Nothing else in the Bible affirms that China will lead the kings of the east. But the passage in question does state that "the kings of the earth and of the whole world" will be gathered for this battle. China will almost certainly be around during this end-time battle and will inevitably be involved; its economic rise since the 1980s and increasing military spending are consistent with the possibility of China having a major role in the battle.

To further support the China interpretation, some Bible scholars point to Revelation 9:16 which states: "16 And the number of the army of the horsemen were two hundred thousand thousand: and I heard the number of them (KJV)." They note that in the 1970s, the Chinese Red Army[239] including militias reportedly numbered 200 million people. However, Revelation 16 makes no reference to the size of the armies led by the kings of the east.

Moreover, in terms of population sizes, China is not the only eastern nation to have a robust headcount. China's population size grew steadily from the late-1300s to the mid-1800s. The population grew most rapidly from 1749 to 1850 when it more than doubled; and from 1960 to

---

[239] That is, the armed forces of the Communist Party of China

2015, the population doubled to nearly 1.4 billion.[240] For much of history, China has had the largest population of any country in the world. However, with its growth rate in decline, China is expected to lose that title—if it hasn't already.

China's nearest rival in this category is India. In 2015, the United Nations predicted that India would become the most populous nation by the year 2022.[241] But in May 2017, *The New York Times* reported that India's population might already be more populous than China. India had grown to 1.33 billion people in 2016, when China's population might have numbered only 1.29 billion (contrary to the Chinese government's estimate of 1.38 billion).[242]

The biblical "kings of the east" could equally be India or China. It is highly improbable that China could now, in the early twenty-first century, mobilize another army of 200 million. The army of "two hundred thousand thousand" from Revelations 9:16 must include more than China. This will be further discussed in Chapter 8 regarding the Antichrist and the Armageddon War.

---

[240] Judith Banister, 1992, "A Brief History of China's Population," in Poston D.L., Yaukey D. (eds) *The Population of Modern China. The Plenum Series on Demographic Methods and Population Analysis.* Springer, Boston, MA, available from https://link.springer.com/chapter/10.1007/978-1-4899-1231-2_3

[241] Sania Farooqui, 2015 July 30, "India Will Become the World's Most Populous Country by 2022, the U.N. Says," retrieved from time.com/3978175/india-population-worlds-most-populous-country/

[242] Chris Buckley, 2017 May 24, "Expert Doubts China's Population Number, Saying India May Be No. 1," retrieved from https://www.nytimes.com/2017/05/24/world/asia/china-india-population.html

China's official government estimates have occasionally been cast into doubt. See for example Irene B. Taeuber, "China's Population: Riddle of the Past, Enigma of the Future," *The Antioch Review*, Vol. 17, No. 1 (Spring, 1957), pp. 7-18, available from http://www.jstor.org/stable/4609926

From the Land of Sinim

There is another Bible passage that most Bible scholars have neglected in interpreting end-time prophecies, namely Isaiah 49:9–13:

> 9 That thou mayest say to the prisoners, Go forth; to them that are in darkness, Shew yourselves. They shall feed in the ways, and their pastures shall be in all high places.
>
> 10 They shall not hunger nor thirst; neither shall the heat nor sun smite them: for he that hath mercy on them shall lead them, even by the springs of water shall he guide them.
>
> 11 And I will make all my mountains a way, and my highways shall be exalted.
>
> 12 Behold, these shall come from far: and, lo, these from the north and from the west; and these from the land of Sinim.
>
> 13 Sing, O heavens; and be joyful, O earth; and break forth into singing, O mountains: for the Lord hath comforted his people, and will have mercy upon his afflicted. (KJV)

There are varying translations of the final word in verse 12. The end of verse 12 in the King James Version, the New American Standard Bible, other versions that favour literal word-for-word translation, as well as several commentaries,[243] refer to people coming from the land of "Sinim." In contrast, the New International Version—which favours less-literal, thought-for-thought translation—refers to people "from the region of Aswan." A few other translations including the English Standard Version—which is somewhat less literal than the KJV or NASB—refer to people from the land of "Syene."

The original Hebrew version "סינים" is pronounced as "seen-EEM." In modern Hebrew, "סינים" and its root word "סין" (pronounced as "seen") mean "China." The full version "סינים" can also mean

---

[243] See for example http://biblehub.com/commentaries/isaiah/49-12.htm

"Chinese."[244] Correspondingly, the Chinese Union Version of the Bible translates "סִינִים" as " 秦國" (Qin Country) which is pronounced as "cheen-gwo." "Qin Country" means the country of the Qin dynasty—i.e., China. As noted at the outset of this chapter, the Qin dynasty unified China by 221 BC. Since that time, the large far east nation has been called "China" or "Sina."

Some scholars reject the interpretation of "סִינִים" to mean China because Isaiah was written in the eighth century BC when Qin country was a small unremarkable place, and long before the Qin dynasty and the name "China."[245] But back in the 1800s, the Bible scholar Heinrich Friedrich Wilhelm offered that a similar-sounding name might have existed among other ancient Middle Eastern languages:

This very ancient and celebrated people was known to the Arabians and Syrians by the name Sin, Tein, Tshini; and a Hebrew writer might well have heard of them, especially if sojourning in Babylon, the metropolis as it were of all Asia.[246]

The website KJV Today offers another solution: "If Isaiah was able to prophetically call the future king Cyrus by his name (Isaiah 44:28, 45:1), it would not have been unusual for Isaiah to have referred to the name of a future nation." And critics who reject the English word Sinim

---

[244] See for example "China in Other Languages," http://www.101languages.net/countries/china-in-other-languages/
"How to pronounce " https://forvo.com/word/%D7%A1%D7%99%D7%9F/#he
"How to say "Chinese" in Hebrew," http://www.dictionary.co.il/hebrew_word.php?topic=h3301&image=h33/h3301005&name=Chinese
Google translation of "" https://translate.google.com/#iw/en/%D7%A1%D7%99%D7%9F

[245] "'Sinim' or 'Syrene/Aswan' in Isaiah 49:12?" retrieved from www.kjvtoday.com/home/sinim-or-syreneaswan-in-isaiah-4912

[246] As quoted in Albert Barnes' Notes on the Bible, regarding Isaiah 49:12, available at biblehub.com/commentaries/isaiah/49-12.htm

"completely destroy Isaiah's prophecy concerning the establishment of China."[247]

The NIV word "Aswan" and the ESV word "Syene" refer to the same city in Egypt; the name changed over time. Those who favour the word "Sinim" note that the verse in question (Isaiah 49:12) refers first to people who "shall come from afar," then to people "from the north and from the west." Since Egypt directly neighbours Israel and Aswan is southwest of Israel, those criteria rule out the Aswan/Syene translation.

Additionally, the principal of Far East Bible College (Singapore) points out the NIV's internal inconsistency: "The word for "Aswan" according to the NIV in Ezekiel 29:10 and 30:6 is סונה."[248] The same internal inconsistency applies to the ESV's use of "Syene."

Isaiah 49:9–11 foretell the Lord's deliverance to prisoners and people in darkness. The verses promise sustenance, guidance, and a clear path. Verse 12 speaks of the people's geographic origins. Verse 13 rejoices in the Lord's comfort and mercy. God has promised amazing blessings to the people of the land of Sinim.

This promise must be fulfilled before the Battle of Armageddon and more importantly before Christ's second coming.

Verse 9 says prisoners (or "those who are bound" in the NASB) will be set free and those who are in darkness will be able to come out of the darkness. In terms of the Sinim/China interpretation, people have already been set free from a five-thousand-year-old bondage to ancestral worship, the one-thousand-year-old legacy of foot binding, and geopolitical adversity such as the "century of humiliation."

---

[247] "'Sinim' or 'Syrene/Aswan' in Isaiah 49:12?" retrieved from www.kjvtoday.com/home/sinim-or-syreneaswan-in-isaiah-4912

[248] Timothy Tow, 1996 July, "NIV Turns "Land of Sinim" Into "Region of Aswan" by a Twist of the Ball-Pen!" retrieved from www.febc.edu.sg/v15/article/def_niv_turns_land_of_sinim

Chinese Christian Growth Bombshell

In 1996, Rodney Stark published *The Rise of Christianity*. The book suggests that the Christian church grew 40 percent per decade from the year AD 40 to AD 300 when there were 6.3 million believers, accounting for 10.5 percent of the Roman empire.[249]

Could Christianity spread at such an explosive rate in modern-day China? How much has it already grown since 1949 when the Communist (antireligious) leadership took over?

If there were one million Christians in China in 1949, a growth rate of 40 percent per decade would see 10.5 million believers by 2019. Adopting a more aggressive growth rate of 93 percent per decade, one million in 1949 would explode to 70 million Christians by 2019. These numbers may seem unrealistically high, but in a population of over 1.3 billion the figure of 70 million Christians in China is a very conservative estimate.

In 2011, China's Pu Shi Institute for Social Science examined Henan Province, one of over thirty provinces in China. They found that the number of Christians in Henan had grown from 70,000 in 1949 to 17 million in 2011, an increase of almost 243 fold (or 24,300 percent). The Institute described the pace of growth as "extremely alarming."[250]

Christianity has spread through all echelons of Chinese society, and this despite state-imposed restrictions on religious practice. The growth is all the more astonishing since missionaries were no longer welcome as of the Communist takeover in 1949. Christianity has grown more than twice as fast in modern-day China as it did under Roman rule from AD 40 to AD 300.

---

[249] Chapter 1 available at http://pdfs.semanticscholar.org/0b25/69e80aa6e07caee275a e6bf619f33ea563cd.pdf

[250] In the original Chinese-language: "河南省从1949年的7万多基督徒，到如今1700多万，六十年增长的速度非常惊人，耐人寻味。" "The Origin and Development of Family Churches in Henan Province," 2011 February 25, retrieved from http://www.pacilution.com/ShowArticle.asp?ArticleID=2830

The Institute's English-language website is at http://www.pacilution.org/english/ShowClass2ad82.html?ClassID=77

This principal author believes that before too long, China will become the nation with the world's largest number of born-again Christians. An aggressive growth rate of 93 percent per decade implies that the Christian population of China has almost doubled in every decade since Mao took power in China and tried turning China into an atheistic nation. Perhaps God has a special purpose for the rise of the Chinese church and nation during this end-time wait for Christ's return.

Korean Christian Growth Bombshell

This principal author is not only excited about the growth of Christianity in China but he is also excited about a possible "unification" of the two Koreas. As North Korea opens up, one can be sure that the North Korean church will explode in its growth. The South Korean church already sends the second-highest number of missionaries into the world. Unification or conciliation between the two Koreas can only prompt the Korean missionary force to ramp up its efforts.

In 2009, investment firm Goldman Sachs published a study on a "United Korea."[251] The study concluded:

- The North Korean economy is at a crossroads: growth has stagnated and the planned system is near collapse, but it has large untapped potential, including rich human capital and abundant mineral resources (valued at around 140 times 2008 GDP).
- The GDP of a united Korea in USD terms could exceed that of France, Germany, and possibly Japan in thirty to forty years, should the growth potential of North Korea, notably its rich mineral wealth, be realized.

---

[251] Goohoon Kwon, Global Economics Paper No: 188, 2009 September, "A United Korea? Reassessing North Korea Risks (Part I)," Goldman Sachs Global Economics, Commodities and Strategy Research, available from www.nkeconwatch.com/nk-uploads/global_economics_paper_no_188_final.pdf

- A gradual integration between the North and South, similar to the pattern followed in China-Hong Kong, is more likely than an instant German-style unification.

Modern Silk Road (Back to Jerusalem) Bombshell

In September 2013, China's President Xi Jinping unveiled the Belt and Road Initiative[252] (originally named One Belt and One Road). It is inspired by the ancient network of East-West trade routes. As Christianity continues to grow in China and Korea, this modern Silk Road initiative will facilitate the work of Eastern multitudes bringing the gospel through unreached people groups and ultimately toward Jerusalem.

As we anticipate the coming Armageddon and Christ's return, may God help us to see His glory in the rise of China, Korea, and many people groups in Asia and Africa that were formerly unreached. God is pouring out His abundant blessings so that people of many more nations will enjoy Christ's second coming.

These Middle Kingdom and Korean bombshells can expedite the gospel's spread to the uttermost parts of the world. With the dual superpower influence of the US and China, followed by Korea, the gospel should soon be brought back to Jerusalem!

One should take heed of the hastening footsteps that are ushering in His second coming. He is coming back soon. Amen, come, Lord Jesus!

---

[252] "Chronology of China's Belt and Road Initiative," updated 2015 March 28, retrieved from http://english.gov.cn/news/top_news/2015/04/20/content_28147 5092566326.htm

CHAPTER 8

THE BREXIT, TEN-KINGS COALITION, AND ANTICHRIST BOMBSHELLS

The Brexit Bombshell

Four decades after joining the former European Economic Community, in 2016 the United Kingdom (UK) held a referendum on whether to stay in or leave the subsequently transformed twenty-eight-member European Union (EU).[253] The referendum on "Brexit" (short for "Britain exiting the European Union") took place on June 23, 2016.

On the eve of the referendum, this principal author spoke in a Chinese church in Milton Keynes, UK, regarding the political and economic prospects of China, the US, and the world at large, as seen through the lens of biblical prophecy and contemporary trends (从圣经和大趋势看中、美与世界政、经前景). After the talk, the wife of a local pastor asked what would happen with the next day's Brexit referendum. Although all the polls on Brexit referendum indicated that the 'no' (stay

---

[253] European Union, "The EU in brief," https://europa.eu/european-union/about-eu/eu-in-brief_en

in EU) vote would prevail, this author replied: Looking rationally at the economic and political consequences of Brexit, there was hardly any reason for the UK to move away from the EU. However, from the perspective of biblical prophecy, the UK must exit the EU. The following day's vote delivered a narrow victory in favour of leaving the EU.[254] This Brexit bombshell caught many political pundits and pollsters by surprise.

More than two years later, in November 2018, BBC News reported that "EU leaders agree UK's Brexit deal at Brussels summit."[255] This report further outlined:

> EU leaders have approved an agreement on the UK's withdrawal and future relations - insisting it is the "best and only deal possible".
>
> After 20 months of negotiations, the 27 leaders gave the deal their blessing after less than an hour's discussion.
>
> They said the deal - which needs to be approved by the UK Parliament - paved the way for an "orderly withdrawal".
>
> Theresa May said the deal "delivered for the British people" and set the UK "on course for a prosperous future".

What led this principal author to think of Brexit as a necessary component of What Might Take Place After This?

The biblical analysis stems from a seemingly unrelated matter—that of the Antichrist.

Who is the Antichrist and what are his characteristics?

---

[254] See for example "Brexit timeline: UK's departure from the EU," 2018 March 26, https://www.bbc.com/news/uk-politics-43546199

[255] https://www.bbc.com/news/uk-46334649

- The Antichrist will appear in the final days—1 John 2:18
  (it is the last hour; and just as you heard that Antichrist is
  coming....);
- There are many Antichrists or deceivers—1 John 2:18 (even
  now many Antichrists have appeared)—1 John 4:3 (every spirit
  that does not confess Jesus is God; this is the spirit of the
  Antichrist); 2 John 1:7 (many deceivers have gone out into the
  world, those who do not acknowledge Jesus Christ as coming
  in the flesh. This is the deceiver and the Antichrist)
- The Antichrist is already in the world—1 John 4:2 (now it is
  already in the world);
- The Antichrist will have ten horns, representing ten Kings—
  Daniel 7: 19–20 (the fourth beast ... [has] ten horns ... on its
  head); Revelation 13:1 (I saw a beast coming up out of the sea,
  having ten horns); Revelation 17:12 (the ten horns which you
  saw are ten kings);
- He will rise to power as a charismatic, diplomatic, shrewd, and
  deceitful leader who will amaze the world by solving difficult
  geopolitical challenges—Daniel 8:25 (through his shrewdness
  He will cause deceit to succeed by his influence); 2 Cor. 11:13–
  15 (such men are false apostles, deceitful workers), Matthew
  24:24 and Mark 13:22 (false Christs and false prophets will
  arise); Revelation 13:8 (all who dwell on the earth will worship
  him, everyone whose name has not been written ... in the book
  of life);
- The Israelis will trust him as the guarantor of peace in the
  Middle East—Daniel 9:27 (he will make a firm covenant with
  many for one week);
- However, he will betray that peace—Matthew 24:15 and Mark
  13:14, referring to Daniel 9:27 and 11:31 (midway through the
  week of peace he will put an end to God-honouring sacrifice
  and offering, instead setting up an abomination that causes
  desolation);

- He will possess supernatural power—Matthew 24:24 and Mark 13:22 (will show signs and wonders in order to lead astray); Revelation 13:13 (he performs great signs);
- The Antichrist will boast of himself as god—Daniel 11:36-37;
- He will try to annihilate both Jews and the left-behind Christians who accepted Christ after the Rapture—Revelation 13:7;
- He stands against God and His anointed one, Jesus Christ—Daniel 11:36-37;
- His reign will encompass the entire world, and will control all aspects of human life—Revelation 13:12 and 15-17; no doubt modern digital technology can aid him in dominating economic, geopolitical, and other human activities;
- He will gain "authority over every tribe and people and tongue and nation"—Revelation 13:7.

Where does the Antichrist come from?

The Bible does not clearly identify his place of origin. There have been many prophetic interpretations claiming that he will be from Israel, Assyria, Greece, Italy, or elsewhere. But Daniel chapter 11 tells us where the Antichrist does not come from:

- He is not the king of the North, because the king of the North will engage the Antichrist in battle—Daniel 11:40; and rumours from the North will disturb him—Daniel 11:44;
- He is not the king of the South, because the king of the South will engage the Antichrist in battle—Daniel 11:40;
- He is unlikely to be from the East, because rumours from the East will disturb him—Daniel 11:44;
- He is not from the Beautiful Land, because the Antichrist will invade the Beautiful Land—Daniel 11:41;

- He is not from Edom, Moab, Ammon, because the leaders from Edom, Moab, and Amon will be delivered from his hand—Daniel 11:41;
- He is not from Egypt, because Egypt and its hidden treasures will fall into the Antichrist's hand—Daniel 11:42-43;
- He is not from Libya or Cush, because he will gain control over their hidden treasures, and their people will submit to the Antichrist—Daniel 11:43.

By a process of elimination, the West is his only possible place of origin.

In addition to a Western place of origin, Daniel's prophecies indicate that the Antichrist will emerge from amidst a coalition of ten kings:

- Daniel 7:7–8 (I saw a fourth beast that had ten horns; another horn, a little one, came up among them, and three of the first horns were pulled out by the roots before it; and behold, this horn possessed eyes like the eyes of a man and a mouth uttering great boasts.); and
- Daniel 7:19-24 (the fourth beast will be a fourth kingdom on the earth, which will be different from all the other kingdoms and will devour the whole earth and tread it down and crush it; and ten kings will arise from the ten horns on its head; and another will arise after them, and he will be different from the previous ones and will subdue three kings).

The Ten-horned Beast

In Revelation, the apostle John speaks of a ten-horned beast that might be interpreted as being the same as Daniel's ten-horned fourth beast:

- Revelation 13:1–2 (I saw a beast coming up out of the sea, having ten horns and seven heads, and on his horns were ten diadems, and on his heads were blasphemous names)— the beast's diadems (jewelled headpieces symbolizing royalty[256]) indicate that the ten-nation coalition will dominate politically;
- Revelation 17:3 (I saw a woman sitting on a scarlet beast, full of blasphemous names, having seven heads and ten horns);
- Revelation 17:7 (the mystery of the woman and of the beast that carries her, which has the seven heads and the ten horns); and
- Revelation 17:12–16 (The ten horns are ten kings who have not yet received a kingdom, but they receive authority as kings with the beast for one hour. These have one purpose, and they give their power and authority to the beast; the ten horns which you saw, and the beast, will hate the harlot).

Ten-kings Coalition

To what extent does the EU match the description of a Western, ten-king coalition? At a minimum, the following factors should be considered.

Firstly, until the UK officially exits, the EU counts twenty-eight member states—too many to match the Bible's prophetic ten-king coalition. Could Brexit be the first of many departures from the EU which whittle down its membership until ten states remain? Currently there is no indication that Brexit will begin such a downward trend.

In June 2017, one year after the Brexit referendum, the US-based Pew Research Center found that few among other European citizens wished for their country to depart the EU. Rather, polls found that Europeans had more favourable views toward the EU compared to a year earlier when the UK was verging on its referendum.[257] Almost two

---

[256] Oxford Dictionary, https://en.oxforddictionaries.com/definition/diadem

[257] Bruce Stokes, Richard Wike, and Dorothy Manevich, 2017 June 15, "Post-Brexit, Europeans More Favorable Toward EU," www.pewglobal.org/2017/06/15/post-brexit-europeans-more-favorable-toward-eu/

years after the Brexit referendum, in May 2018 a Bloomberg financial writer declared that while "Leavers hoped to start a continent-wide revolution," Brexit has become a non-issue for the other EU countries. Other continental concerns have come into view, and Brexit has fallen out of the limelight:[258]

For now, Brexit is more an exception than the start of a trend.

Some Brexiteers had hoped they could "divide and rule" the Union to advance the commercial interests of the UK....

The [other EU membership] has been very disciplined in standing behind its chief negotiator, Michel Barnier.... So far, Barnier has succeeded in obtaining pretty much everything he was aiming for, including ... a steep exit bill.

Secondly, in terms of the political dominance of the ten-king coalition, there too the EU appears to fall short. Granted, some EU members want to strengthen the organization. A few days after the Brexit referendum, on June 27, 2016 the Polish public broadcaster Telewizja Polska published a leaked German-French plan for "A strong Europe in a world of uncertainties."[259] The German-French document observed:

The British case is unique. But ... support and passion for our common project has faded over the last decade in parts of our societies....

However, *The Economist* reports that The EU's popularity ratings in other member countries received a slight boost from the Brexit decision, but they remain strikingly low by past standards; John Peet, 2017 March 25, "Creaking at 60: The future of the European Union," https://www.economist.com/special-report/2017/03/25/the-future-of-the-european-union

[258] Ferdinando Giugliano, 2018 May 25, Europe Is Ready to Move On from Brexit, https://www.bloomberg.com/news/articles/2018-05-25/europe-is-ready-to-move-on-from-brexit

[259] 2016 June 27, "Europejskie superpaństwo. Zobacz oryginalny dokument," https://www.tvp.info/25939587/europejskie-superpanstwo-zobacz-oryginalny-dokument

France and Germany will ... promote a more coherent and a more assertive Europe on the world stage.

Superstate Plan

The German-French document—which some news outlets character-ized as a "superstate" plan[260]—proposed greater military coordination; a unified European policy on asylum and migration, and "the world's first multinational border and coast guard" and joint databases of migrant information; and continued use of "the euro [common currency, which] reflects our commitment to the irreversibility of European integration."

Similarly, in September 2017, France24 reported that French President Emmanuel Macron—who took office in April 2017 after the German-French leak—spoke of the EU's necessity and proposed military integration, intelligence-sharing, joint border enforcement, and market integration:[261]

> With [security as] the "first" priority and Europe facing the "progressive disengagement of the US" as well as a "sustainable terrorist phenomenon," Macron proposed a "common interven-tion force, common budget, and common doctrine to act." He also proposed bringing soldiers from across Europe into national armies, vowing to "welcome into the French army soldiers from all over Europe."

---

[260] See for example https://www.express.co.uk/news/politics/683739/EU-referendum-German-French-European-superstate-Brexit

and https://www.news.com.au/finance/economy/world-economy/britain-dodges-european-union-superstate-bullet-with-plans-revealed-days-after-brexit-vote/news-story/76973491f4063530d83d0e4780c8cb9b

[261] France24, 2017 September 26, "French President Macron presents vision of post-Brexit Europe," www.france24.com/en/20170926-live-french-president-macron-presents-vision-post-brexit-europe-eu-germany-election#

In a move that bodes well for the EU's future, in November 2017 it was announced that twenty-three member states had signed up for permanent structured cooperation (PESCO) on security and defence.[262] With PESCO on security and defence, each signatory nation would contribute military capabilities; they would also benefit from a European Defence Fund of money for research and purchases.[263] Some news outlets reported the dawn of an EU mega-army,[264] but a BBC journalist explained that PESCO on security and defence does not create a jointly-controlled army. Rather, member states continue to have authority over when and where to deploy their military resources:

> There is no "European army," in the same sense that there is actually no "NATO army." It simply means that national military capabilities that exercise together can be brought under a single command at a time of crisis.

The UK tabloid *Express* noted a link between PESCO and the German-French commitment to European integration: "Long blocked by Britain, which feared the creation of an EU army, defence integration was revived by France and Germany after last June's Brexit vote."[265]

---

[262] Council of the EU, 2017 November 13, "Defence cooperation: 23 member states sign joint notification on the Permanent Structured Cooperation (PESCO)," www.consilium.europa.eu/en/press/press-releases/2017/11/13/defence-cooperation-23-member-states-sign-joint-notification-on-pesco/
The UK did not sign on, since it plans to exit the EU See for example BBC News, 2017 November 13, "European Union gives impetus to joint defence plan," https://www.bbc.com/news/world-europe-41971867

[263] See for example BBC News, 2017 November 13, "European Union gives impetus to joint defence plan," https://www.bbc.com/news/world-europe-41971867

[264] See for example http://www.businessinsider.com/eu-countries-agree-mega-army-2017-11
and https://www.express.co.uk/news/world/878918/eu-army-european-defence-union-pact-brussels-uk-brexit

[265] Joey Millar, 2017 November 13, "Official DAWN OF EU ARMY: Brussels signs off military plan & hails historic day without UK," https://www.express.co.uk/news/world/878918/eu-army-european-defence-union-pact-brussels-uk-brexit

Military/defence integration could serve as an important foundation to support the rise of a strong, globally dominating Antichrist.

On the other side of the balance, however, is a level of dissatisfaction with the EU's status quo. The aforementioned June 2017 study by Pew Research Center found that many Europeans want their national governments to have a greater say.

Paradox of Progress

Every four years concurrent with the US presidential election, the US National Intelligence Council (NIC) publishes a strategic projection of how key trends and issues might shape the world for the following twenty years. The NIC's Global Trends report of December 2016/ January 2017, titled *Paradox of Progress*,[266] foresees a shaky future for the EU:

- The EU will be absorbed by questions of governance, internal divisions, and economic struggles which will threaten its status as a global player;[267] and
- "The post-World War II international order ... is in question as power diffuses globally, shuffling seats at the table of international decision making."[268]

Thus the EU might not have the global dominance that will characterize the ten-king coalition.

Revelation 17:12–13 offers a third and fourth factor by which to assess the EU's conformity with the prophetic ten-king coalition:

---

[266] National Intelligence Council, 2017 January, *Paradox of Progress*, https://www.dni.gov/index.php/global-trends-home

[267] NIC, 2017, *Paradox of Progress*, p.33

[268] NIC, 2017, *Paradox of Progress*, p.43

12 The ten horns which you saw are ten kings who have not yet received a kingdom, but they receive authority as kings with the beast for one hour. 13 These have one purpose, and they give their power and authority to the beast. (NASB)

Verse 12 indicates that the ten kings will only receive authority for a brief time.[269] This appears to rule out the EU in favour of a subsequent Western coalition that will grow to ten members at a later date.

Verse 13 indicates that the ten kings will share the common purpose of propping up the Antichrist, and in some sense they will conspire to that end.[270] However, EU nations are rarely of one mind. For example, the aforementioned Bloomberg article stated:

[Even as they have united behind the EU's negotiator on Brexit proceedings,] Differences among the remaining EU states exist, and more may emerge over time. Germany and Italy are said to be more open to a compromise, mainly to preserve trade links, while France has taken the hardest line, probably to lure away investments now in Britain.[271]

Those who are committed to the EU project have found it necessary to expressly remind their neighbours to remain on board:

Whenever the likes of Macron or German Chancellor Angela Merkel give a speech, it is typically to remind Britain that "divide and rule" will be a failing strategy. "Let us stay united. Don't let anyone drive a wedge between us," said Merkel in a speech in Berlin last year [in 2017].[272]

---

[269] See for example Barnes' Notes on the Bible, Jamieson-Fausset-Brown Bible Commentary, and Meyer's NT Commentary, available from biblehub.com/commentaries/revelation/17-12.htm

[270] See for example Barnes' Notes on the Bible, Jamieson-Fausset-Brown Bible Commentary, and Geneva Study Bible, available from biblehub.com/commentaries/revelation/17-13.htm

[271] European Union, "The EU in brief," https://europa.eu/european-union/about-eu/eu-in-brief_en

[272] European Union, "The EU in brief," https://europa.eu/european-union/about-eu/eu-in-brief_en

While the EU might not as yet fit the bill of the prophetic Western ten-king coalition, it might be the precursor.

The EU's own precursor was a six-member European Economic Community formed in March 1957 in order to increase economic cooperation among member nations. The underlying premise is that economic cooperation leads to interdependence and thus militates in favour of harmony rather than conflict.[273] Over time the organization moved beyond economics to deal with policy matters including environment, security, and migration; in 1993 its name changed to European Union to reflect its broadened scope.[274] By 2013, the EU had grown to twenty-eight members with more potential applicants lined up.

Possibility of Multi-tier / Multi-speed EU

In March 2017, a white paper by the European Commission (the EU's executive branch[275]) acknowledged that the EU must consider adapting to address challenges and criticisms:

> Many Europeans consider the Union as either too distant or too interfering in their day-to-day lives. Others question its added-value ... [and] Europe's challenges show no sign of abating.

The Commission proposed five possible trajectories for the EU moving forward.[276] In "Scenario 3: Those who want more do more," the EU

---

[273] European Union, "The EU in brief," https://europa.eu/european-union/about-eu/eu-in-brief_en

[274] European Union, "The EU in brief," https://europa.eu/european-union/about-eu/eu-in-brief_en

[275] The European Commission proposes and enforces legislation and implements EU policies and the budget. See for example European Commission, https://europa.eu/european-union/about-eu/institutions-bodies/european-commission_en

[276] European Commission, 2017 March, *White paper on the future of Europe: Reflections and scenarios for the EU27 by 2025*, https://ec.europa.eu/commission/white-paper-future-europe_en

"allows willing member states to do more together in specific areas." All EU members would carry on with the single market for trade, but each state would have discretion to work more closely together in other domains (e.g. taxation, migration, security, foreign policy, defence, social matters, etc.)

The Economist supported this trajectory, which it described as a "multi-speed" Europe:

> What is really needed is ... to drop the rigid one-size-fits-all model.
>
> A union of twenty-eight ... is very different from the original club of six. There are countless examples of opt-outs from common policies, ranging from large ones (common security and defence policy or Schengen) to minor ones (controls on purchases by foreigners of houses ... rules for ... selling alcohol). In this sense, a multi-speed, multi-tier union exists already.[277]

In addition to opt-out clauses, the Treaty on EU[278] provides for the aforementioned PESCO (permanent structured cooperation) on security and defence.

Morever, since the 1990s, the Treaty on EU[279] and the Treaty on the Functioning of the EU[280] (TFEU) have provided for "enhanced cooperation" among a subgroup of willing member states. Article 329 of the TFEU provides that member states wishing to establish enhanced cooperation between themselves must request approval from either the

---

[277] 2017 March 25, Creaking at 60: The future of the European Union, https://www.economist.com/special-report/2017/03/25/the-future-of-the-european-union
  See also 2017 March 23, "Differentiate or bust: Europe's future is multi-speed and multi-tier," https://www.economist.com/special-report/2017/03/23/europes-future-is-multi-speed-and-multi-tier

[278] Articles 42(6) and 46, and Protocol 10

[279] Article 20

[280] Article 326-334

European Commission or the European Council,[281] depending on the area of cooperation. Of particular relevance for students of Bible prophecy, Article 20(2) of the Treaty on EU provides:

> The decision authorising enhanced cooperation shall be adopted by the Council as a last resort, when it has established that the objectives of such cooperation cannot be attained within a reasonable period by the Union as a whole, and provided that at least nine Member States participate in it.... [Underline added.]

One way for the Antichrist to rise out of a ten-king coalition would emerge if a subgroup of ten EU members (enough to surpass the minimum requirement of nine) sought enhanced cooperation and—thereby forming a ten-king coalition regarding a specific subject matter.

Germany, France, the European Commission, and the NIC agree that contemporary geopolitics create many challenges for governing institutions like the EU. It is plausible that global instability might overwhelm even a distilled subgroup of ten EU members engaged in enhanced cooperation—and that the Antichrist might take advantage of the instability to seize control of the ten-nation coalition as a step toward conquering the world at large.

Given the following report, the possible formation of an EU Army is not too far off: On November 2018, the *Independent* publishd the headline: "EU army: Brussels 'delighted' that Angela Merkel and Macron want to create European military force"[282]:

> The European Commission has said it is "delighted" that the leaders of France and Germany have backed the creation of a

---

[281] The European Council is the highest site of political cooperation among EU members. The Counsil defines the EU's general political direction and priorities, but does not make laws. See for example "European Council," https://europa.eu/european-union/about-eu/institutions-bodies/european-council_en

[282] https://www.independent.co.uk/news/world/europe/eu-army-angela-merkel-macron-germany-france-military-european-commission-juncker-a8633196.html

"real" EU army. A spokesperson for the commission's president Jean-Claude Juncker said he was "pleased" that the argument for the force seemed to be "going in our direction".

Addressing the European Parliament on Tuesday Angela Merkel said she supported a "real, true" European army, echoing an identical call by her French counterpart Emmanuel Macron the week before.

What Might Happen After This—Possible Islamization of EU

Chapter 5 examines seven sets of biblical passages relating to Babylon. Many of these passages can likewise be applied to possible Islamization of the EU.

In December 2016, the Center for the Study of Political Islam International (CSPI) published an analysis titled: *Islamic Saturation of Countries: A Critical Point*. The study highlighted:[283]

> We look at today's Islamic countries - Iraq, Egypt, Turkey, Lebanon, North Africa, Iran, Afghanistan and Pakistan. These all used to have civilizations that were Christian, Hindu, Buddhist and Zoroastrian but are all now completely Islamic.
>
> Historical data suggests that without violence or external forces, no countries recovered from becoming completely Islamized after crossing this critical point of 10%.
>
> Our study projects that Germany, Belgium, UK, Sweden and Netherlands have only 7 to 17 years from now until the 10% of Muslim population is reached. France has already reached this critical point around 2015.

---

[283] *file:///D:/0.0%202018okokokrapture/islamizatio.pdf*

If Christians are raptured to meet the Lord prior to the Tribulation on earth,[284] it is likely that Islam will become the most important and powerful religion among people who remain on earth. Islam's influence would pervade the ten-king coalition, and the would-be Antichrist might grasp the opportunity to align himself with Islam—thus rendering himself as a platform on which the Islamic-based harlot might sit (see Revelation 17:3 and 7, noted above; see also Chapter 5).

Perhaps the leader from the ten-king coalition might allow Islamic leaders to impose the Islamic calendar[285] and Islamic laws (see Daniel 7:25), thus providing for unrestrained power to slaughter 'infidels' around the world.

What Might Happen After This—Possible EU Superstate

Based on the above, one could speculate as to What Might Happen After This:

- Perhaps as the US withdraws from both the Middle East and Europe (see Chapter 2) and the Lord defeats Russia and Iran (see Chapters 3 and 5) in the Gog-Magog invasion of the Holy Land, a strong political leader might rise from the ten-king coalition to exploit the geopolitical vacuum in both the Middle East and Europe.
- Perhaps the ten-king coalition might become a European

---

[284] Some believe that the Rapture will remove Christians from the earth before the Tribulation. Others believe that Christians will remain on the earth during the Tribulation and the Rapture will take place at Christ's second coming.

[285] Unlike the solar-based Gregorian calendar (365.242189 days per year), the Islamic calendar has 354 or 355 days per year, beginning from AD 622 when the prophet Mohammed migrated to Medina. January 1, 2019 would land in the fourth month of the Islamic year 1440. See for example "The Islamic Calendar," https://www.timeanddate.com/calendar/islamic-calendar.html and "How Accurate Are Calendars?" https://www.timeanddate.com/date/perfect-calendar.html

superstate with unified economic, military, and political structures.

- Perhaps the Islamic holy site of the Dome of the Rock could be destroyed during the Gog-Magog war, making way for Israelis to build the Third Temple on this site (see Chapter 4).

- Perhaps with peaceful overtures between Arab nations and Israel (see Chapter 5), some Arab nations might refrain from supporting a Russian-Iranian invasion of the Holy Land in the Gog–Magog war (see Chapters 3 and 5). A would-be Antichrist could take advantage of the situation and establish a temporary peace over Israel (see Daniel 9:27, noted above).

- Perhaps advancements in producing oil and gas might make Israel an energy superpower in the Middle East (see Chapter 3). And a shrewd leader from the ten-king coalition might seek favour with the new energy superpower by somehow negotiating a peace treaty for the Middle East (see Daniel 9:27, noted above) and convincing Arab states to allow Israel to build the Third Temple (see Chapter 4).

- Perhaps the Rapture will take place, whereby Christians will rise from the earth and meet the Lord in the air (1 Thessalonians 4:16–17). Perhaps countries such as the US, the UK, China, and Korea, having suddenly lost a large percentage of their populations during the Rapture, might be crippled to the point of having little if any influence regarding the Antichrist's self-promoting agenda

- Perhaps the leader from the ten-king coalition will declare himself as a deity and reveal himself as the Antichrist—placing him in direct confrontation with the Islamic-based harlot, the Jews, as well as left-behind Christians.[286]

- Perhaps the Antichrist will gain worldwide economic control

---

[286] In Matthew 24:40–41, Jesus warns that when he returns, "Then shall two be in the field; the one shall be taken, and the other left. Two women shall be grinding at the mill; the one shall be taken, and the other left." (KJV)

and limiting market access to those who bear the mark of the beast's name or number (Revelation 13:16–18).

- Perhaps as this Antichrist tries dominating global geopolitics, resistance forces might oppose him and lead 200 million troops against him (Revelation 9:16 NASB). The resistance forces might come from the east (Revelation 16:12), as part of the nations that will take part in the battle of Armageddon (Revelation 16:14).
- In the battle of Armageddon, the Antichrist will "cause astounding devastation" (Daniel 8:24 NIV). A fourth of the earth will perish (Revelation 6:8).
- Perhaps the disastrous battle of Armageddon and his frustration with the domineering Islamic-based harlot will motivate the Antichrist to hate the harlot, make her desolate and naked, eat her flesh and burn her with fire (Revelation 17:16).
- At the height of the battle of Armageddon, Christ will return and the Antichrist will be slain "with the breath of his mouth" (2 Thessalonians 2:8), "destroyed forever" (Daniel 7:26 NIV and NASB), and thrown into "the burning sulfur" (Revelation 20:10 NIV and ESV).

This principal author is convinced that What Might Take Place After This will involve an EU-based superstate, to provide the political basis for the rise of the Antichrist.

And why does this principle Author think Brexit is part of What Might Take Place After This? The coming formation of an EU-based superstate is one of the foremost considerations:

- The UK has steadfastly refused to surrender its currency in favor of the Euro, and to surrender its customs and border control. As such, the UK is unlikely to be willing to become an integral part of EU-based superstate or EU-controlled army, which will eventually become the Ten-kings Coalition.

- Given the way the UK citizens cherish their monarchy, the UK is unlikely to surrender the monarchy in favor of the EU based superstate.

- Despite the Christian church's diminishing influence in the UK's socio-political realm, UK citizens could reinvigorate the notion of 'God saves the Queen' as a national motto in resisting 'Islamization.' May God save the Queen.

- Although there remains uncertainty on whether there will be hard or soft Brexit, or when Brexit might take place, eventually history is HIS STORY. If the push for Brexit continues, Britain will ultimately leave the EU and will be unlikely to join the ten-kings coalition.

- As ten EU members seek to bypass the organization's large and unwieldy nature by pursuing enhanced cooperation on a specific subject matter, the ground will be prepared for the rise of the Antichrist. But Daniel 7:26 and Revelation 17:14 state that the Lord will ultimately vanquish the "ten-King coalition" and the Antichrist who arose from it:

- Daniel 7:26 (the judgment shall sit, and the newly-emerged king's dominion will be taken away, annihilated and destroyed forever); and

- Revelation 17:14 (the ten kings will wage war against the Lamb, and the Lamb will overcome them, because He is Lord of lords and King of kings).

We should be alert and prepared for the ensuing Rapture and Tribulation. He is coming back soon. Amen. Come, Lord Jesus!

CHAPTER 9

THE BOMBSHELLS LEADING TO THE GRAND RETURN OF JESUS CHRIST

Fulfilled Prophecies in Jesus' Olivet Discourse

Matthew 24, Mark 13, and Luke 21 each recount Jesus's prophetic remarks regarding the end of this world and his own second coming (sometimes known as the Olivet Discourse, since Jesus was speaking from the Mount of Olives). Jesus knew that his time on earth would soon end, so it was imperative that he talk not only about the temple's forthcoming destruction but more importantly about what would happen at the end of the age leading up to his return.

His disciples would have been taken aback by the bombshell prediction that the Jewish temple would be destroyed: "Not one stone here will be left on another; every one will be thrown down" (Matthew 24:2, Mark 13:2, Luke 21:6). Right away, the disciples asked for more information:

- When would this happen?
- What would be the sign of Jesus's return?

- And what would be the sign of the end of the age? (Matthew 24:2, Mark 13:4, Luke 21:7).

Two thousand years after the Olivet Discourse, we can see that a portion of Jesus's prophecies have been fulfilled as the time of his grand return draws near.

- The fig tree has budded (Matthew 24:32–33, Mark 13:28–29, Luke 21:30–31)—Jesus describes a fig tree that has become tender and sprouts leaves. Some commentators link the budding fig tree to Israel's reestablishment as a nation.[287] Chapter 4 discusses Israel's 1948 declaration of statehood, its miraculous military successes, and its security against hostile neighbours. Jesus instructs his disciples: "when you see these things happening [the fig tree's budding], recognize that the kingdom of God is near." This suggests that when we see what God has done for Israel, we can be assured that His kingdom is near.

Other Fulfilled End-Time Prophecies

Before moving on to Jesus's other Olivet prophecies, we will take a detour to consider another Bible prophecy related to the end times that has in some measure been fulfilled:

- Human knowledge has grown exponentially, as have speeds and amounts of travel—and some consider this as fulfillment of Daniel 12:14. Daniel 12:4 records a mystery that Daniel

---

[287] See for example Clarence Larkin, 1918, *Dispensational Truth*, chapter 29, available at https://www.blueletterbible.org/study/larkin/dt/29.cfm

and Derek Walker, 2008, The Seven Times of The Gentiles, Chapter 9, available at https://www.oxfordbiblechurch.co.uk/index.php/books/the-seven-times-of-the-gentiles/652-chapter-9-the-parable-of-the-fig-tree-israel-s-fall-and-rise

might not have understood: "But thou, O Daniel, shut up the words, and seal the book, even to the time of the end: many shall run to and fro, and knowledge shall be increased" (KJV). The concept of running to and fro is translated from the Hebrew[288] word ש ו ט ("shoot," shûwt, or šūṭ) which can be defined as pushing forth, figuratively lashing at the sea, and/or by implication travelling about.[289] While some consider this prophecy fulfilled by modern travel which is relatively quick and commonplace, some interpret this figuratively to mean the pursuit of knowledge, and/or the search for knowledge about God. According to Bible teacher John MacArthur, for example, the Hebrew verb form of running to and fro "always refers to the mjmovement of a person searching for something,"[290] not merely traveling about. In terms of the increase in knowledge foreseen in Daniel 12:4, the original Hebrew word רָבָה ("rabah" or rä·vä') means not only addition but rather multiplication; substantial increases in the knowledge.[291] Here again, some believe this applies to the exponential growth of knowledge facilitated by modern technologies, while others interpret this more narrowly to refer to knowledge about the Lord. John MacArthur states that knowledge has been bound up in Daniel's books and in the end times, people will obtain knowledge from those scriptures.

---

[288] The book of Daniel was written in two languages from the same region with similar alphabets; the first chapter and verses 1-3 of chapter 2 in Hebrew, then 2:4 through chapter 7 in Aramaic, and chapters 8 through 12 in Hebrew. See for example Waltter C. Kaiser, Jr., "The Book of Daniel," Lesson 1, https://www.torahclass.com/archived-articles/1230-featured-article-sp-1535435562

[289] *Strong's Exhaustive Concordance*, H7751, available at https://www.blueletterbible.org/lang/lexicon/lexicon.cfm?Strongs=H7751

[290] John MacArthur, 2005, *The MacArthur Bible Commentary* (Nashville: Thomas Nelson), p. 968.

[291] *Strong's Exhaustive Concordance*, H7235, available at https://www.blueletterbible.org/lang/lexicon/lexicon.cfm?Strongs=H7235

Prophecies in Jesus's Olivet Discourse in the Process of Being Fulfilled

Returning to Jesus's Oliver discourse: other aspects of Jesus's prophecies are in the process of being fulfilled in the lead-up to his grand return:

- The gospel is being preached in the whole world (Matthew 24:14, Mark 13:10)—Christian missionaries have worked in all regions of the globe, but some people groups (usually isolated by language and tribe) remain unreached.[292]
- False messiahs and false prophets arise and mislead (Matthew 24:5, 11, 24; Mark 13:6 and 22; Luke 21:8)—Throughout history and even while Jesus's apostles were still alive, false saviours have cropped up in various parts of the world. This will soon culminate in the rise of the Antichrist.
- Wars (Matthew 24:6-7, Mark 13:7, Luke 21:9)—It almost goes without saying that humankind has continuously subjected itself to wars and threats of war; the twentieth century alone included two World Wars and the threat of nuclear annihilation, and the 21st century has experienced vast numbers of human displacement (refugees fleeing war-ravaged nations).
- Earthquakes and famine (Matthew 24:7, Mark 13:8, Luke 21:11)—Earthquakes and famine have occurred throughout history, even in the Old Testament.[293] Famine is often a consequence of war and human policies rather than the inability to produce enough food to support a growing population.[294] Likewise, earthquake risks can also be

---

[292] See for example the Joshua Project's list of 100 Largest Unreached people groups, https://joshuaproject.net/unreached/1

[293] See for example earthquakes in Exodus 19:18 and Numbers 16:31-33; famine in Genesis 41:54 and 2 Samuel 21:1

[294] See for example Cormac O Grada, 2009, *Famine: A Short History* (Princeton University Press)

exacerbated by human responses to global climate change, for example diverting water flows which add pressure to seismic fault lines.[295] The risks of earthquakes and famine are likely to increase as climate change makes it increasingly difficult to make responsible policies and choices.

- Tsunamis, cyclones/hurricanes/typhoons, and other water-based natural disasters (Luke 21:25)—Water-based disasters have occurred throughout history, even in the Old Testament,[296] but as with earthquakes and famine these natural disasters are increasingly likely due to the worldwide effects of climate change.

- Persecution of Christians (Matthew 24:9, Mark 13:11, Luke 21:12)—Just as Jesus himself was rejected, so too Christ's followers have been persecuted throughout the ages. This includes persecution at the hands of atheist communist governments and Islamic powers. With the rise of radical Islamic-based entities (discussed in Chapter 5), the persecution of Christians is likely to intensify in Muslim-dominated countries and in other parts of the world where radicals bring war to 'infidels.'

- Lawlessness and wickedness (Matthew 24:12)—As formerly-Christian-dominated nations embrace more liberal ideologies, legal standards increasingly protect wickedness and wickedness increasingly becomes the social norm.

---

[295] See for example Kristin Hugo, 2017 September 24, "The Weird Way that Climate Change Could Make Earthquakes Worse," www.newsweek.com/weird-way-climate-change-could-make-earthquakes-worse-669922

[296] See for example Noah's flood including Genesis 7:11

Other Bible End Time Prophecies in the Process of Being Fulfilled

As another detour from Jesus's prophecies: other Bible prophecies are also in the process of being fulfilled in relation to the end times:

- As detailed in Chapters 3, 5, and 8, the rise of Russia in the uttermost north, radical Islamic-based entities as Babylon, and a ten-king coalition in Europe all point toward Jesus's coming return.
- As described in Chapter 6, the previously-implausible mixture of iron and clay (diametrically-opposed nations) will precede the coming extraction of a rock without human hands (Daniel 2:34). And this represents Christ's return to earth.

Prophecies in Jesus' Olivet Discourse Have Yet to Be Fulfilled

Again returning to Jesus's Oliver discourse: other prophecies from Jesus's discourse have yet to be fulfilled:

- The abomination that causes desolation will stand in the holy place (Matthew 24:15, Mark 13:14)—Here, Jesus echoes Daniel 9:27, 11:31, and 12:11. While the Old Testament passages have been interpreted to apply to ancient Greek ruler Antiochus Epiphanies who worshiped Zeus in the Jewish temple, and to the first-century Romans who overthrew Jerusalem, these passages might also apply to the Antichrist's future actions. As mentioned in Chapter 8, the abomination that causes desolation will stand in the holy place likely when the Antichrist reveals himself as the Antichrist, midway through the week of peace.

- The great tribulation on earth (Matthew 24:21-22, Mark 13:19-20)—Some believe that the Rapture (1 Thessalonians 4:16-17) will remove Christians from the earth before this period of tribulation, but Jesus's remarks suggest that Christians will remain on earth and those terrible days will be cut short for the sake of believers (Matthew 24:22, Mark 13:20). It is possible that these Christians are 'left-behind Christians' who accepted Christ after believers were taken up to be with the Lord.

Other End-Time Bible Prophecies Have Yet to Be Fulfilled

Beyond Jesus's remarks on the Mount of Olives, we also await the fulfilment of other Bible prophecies related to end-time events:

- As described in Chapter 3, the nation to the uttermost north (Russia) will lead a coalition of Islamic-dominated nations in the Gog-Magog War.
- As discussed in Chapter 4, US President Trump's bold decision to move the US Embassy to Jerusalem is a stepping stone to the prophesied rebuilding of the Third Temple.
- Chapter 8 mentions that the Antichrist might attempt to dominate the global market and limit market access to those who bear the mark of the beast's name or number (Revelation 13:16-18).
- Chapter 7 points to the drying up of the Euphrates River, as foretold in Revelation 16:12–16. Perhaps this could happen as a result of climate change and/or the coming Gog-Magog war.
- Also described in Chapters 7 and 8 is a future Battle of Armageddon (Revelation 16:14, 16).

His Final Victory

At the close of his Olivet discourse, Jesus reassures his believers by forecasting his victory after the tribulation (Matthew 24:29a, Mark 13:24a):

- The sign of the Son of Man will appear in heaven, the people of earth will see him coming on the clouds with power and glory, he will send forth his angels, and he will gather his elect (Matthew 24:30–31, Mark 13:26–27, Luke 21:27).
- Jesus's return will be swift and unpredictable, like lightning (Matthew 24:27).

Other Bible passages also foresee the Lord's return:

- The Lord will return majestically (Revelation 19:11–16).
- The world will belong to the Lord (Revelation 11:15).
- In a final victory, the Antichrist will be subdued and destroyed (Revelation 19:20).
- When Christ takes up his reign over the earth, those who were beheaded due to their testimonies about him and because of God's word will be revived and reign with Christ for a thousand years (Revelation 20:4).

He Is Coming Back Soon

As we see end-times geopolitical bombshells happening all around the world, taking place in accordance with ancient Bible prophecies, we must know that He is coming back soon—His final victory is coming soon! Amen, Lord Jesus!

We must also heed the warning in Revelation 22:18-19 (NASB):

18 I testify to everyone who hears the words of the prophecy of this book: if anyone adds to them, God will add to him the plagues which are written in this book; 19 and if anyone takes away from the words of the book of this prophecy, God will take away his part from the tree of life and from the holy city, which are written in this book.

Finally, in the words of Revelation 22:20 (NASB): "He who testifies to these things says, 'Yes, I am coming quickly.' Amen. Come, Lord Jesus."

CPSIA information can be obtained
at www.ICGtesting.com
Printed in the USA
LVHW081139290120
645173LV00007B/19

9 780310 102045